PRAISE FOR *THE 6-MINUTE WORK DAY*

"Jam-packed with effective strategies you can implement immediately."
—**Chris Widener, Bestselling Author of** *The Art of Influence*

"Douglas Vermeeren has hit this one out of the park. This book is bound to become a classic in personal development literature."
—**Dr. Joe Vitale, Featured Teacher in** *The Secret*

"If you want to achieve more and improve your outcomes, do yourself a favor and read this book."
—**Dr. Greg Reid, Founder of Secret Knock and Author of** *Stickability*, **part of the Think and Grow Rich series**

"Douglas Vermeeren definitely knows what he's talking about."
—**Marci Shimoff, Author of** *Chicken Soup for the Woman's Soul* **and Featured Teacher in** *The Secret*

"Sound business strategies and principles that anyone can apply."
—**Frank Maguire, Cofounder of FedEx**

"Improve your situation and unlock more powerful results in your life."
—**Barnet Bain, Academy Award–Winning Director, Producer of** *What Dreams May Come*

"A true master of business and entrepreneurship. A unique perspective on success that includes essentials previously overlooked."
—**Stefan Aarnio, Award-Winning Real Estate Investor**

THE 6-MINUTE WORK DAY

ALSO BY DOUGLAS VERMEEREN

Personal Power Mastery

*Know Your Audience: 10x Your
Speaking Business*

*Guerrilla Achiever: The Unconventional
Way to Become Highly Successful*

*Guerrilla Millionaire: Unlock the
Secrets of the Self-Made Millionaire*

THE
6-
MINUTE
WORK DAY

AN ENTREPRENEUR'S GUIDE TO USING THE POWER OF LEVERAGE TO CREATE ABUNDANCE AND FREEDOM

DOUGLAS VERMEEREN

Matt Holt Books
An Imprint of BenBella Books, Inc.
Dallas, TX

BenBella Books, Inc.
10440 N. Central Expressway
Suite 800
Dallas, TX 75231
benbellabooks.com
Send feedback to feedback@benbellabooks.com

BenBella is a federally registered trademark
Matt Holt and logo are trademarks of BenBella Books

Printed in the United States of America
10 9 8 7 6 5 4 3 2 1

Library of Congress Control Number: 2021034776
ISBN 9781953295767 (print)
ISBN 9781637740101 (ebook)

Editing by Katie Dickman
Copyediting by Michael Fedison
Proofreading by Greg Teague and Lisa Story
Text design by Katie Hollister
Text composition by Aaron Edmiston
Cover design by Brigid Pearson
Printed by Lake Book Manufacturing

To Markus, Dez, and Baby C

CONTENTS

FOREWORD

SHARON LECHTER

We spend our young lives in school being trained (and programmed) to become employees where we exchange our time and energy for money. This results in us placing our financial health and dependence on our employer. Way too many of us end up living our lives struggling financially, living paycheck to paycheck instead of creating a financial foundation that will help us create the life we deserve. It is very difficult to create the life you want when your financial success is dependent on someone else and/or an hourly wage.

As Douglas shares, "If you look closely, the workday is the foundational concept of trading time for money. In order to survive, we have been taught that we need to put in a nine-to-five day and we need to be prepared for a forty-hour workweek.

In addition (and this is the dreadful part), you need to be prepared to spend most of your life doing it."

Instead of *spending your time* as an employee, I ask
you to consider *investing your time* to buy, build, or create
income-producing assets.

- Are you ready to create wealth?
- Are you tired of working hard and never getting ahead?
- Are you frustrated with watching others create great
  success and feeling like you were left in their dust?
- Are you looking for a different path?
- Are you ready to learn from someone who has *been
  there, done that?*

If your answer to any of these questions is "Yes" . . . then
The 6-Minute Work Day is for you.

First, the book will help you identify where you are trading
or losing your time, and even more importantly, why! Then it
will reveal the steps you can take to reclaim control of your
life and win your time back through the process.

As part of the backstory, when Douglas first asked me
to write the foreword for his new book, I was very honored.
However, when I received the draft, I panicked a bit when I
saw the title, *The 6-Minute Work Day*. My immediate thought
was, *Oh no—he has gone to the dark side and the book is about
getting rich quick.*

And then I started reading. His messaging is brilliant and so very aligned with what I teach. *The 6-Minute Work Day* is the destination he has achieved by applying the principles he shares in the book, and he invites you to join him there.

Douglas shares that *time* is our most precious currency. You can make money, lose it, and then make it back . . . but once time is spent, you can never recover it.

The wealthy do not trade time for money. However, they all do have one thing in common, no matter where they live or what language they speak. They invest their time in buying, building, or creating income-producing assets that will work hard for them. They understand the power of assets!

You are financially free when the income from your assets exceeds your monthly expenses (it does *not* have to be millions of dollars).

If you are ready to win your time back, start focusing on assets. The word *asset* is my favorite word on earth. In fact, one of my initiatives is "ASSETS ARE $EXY!" to highlight the importance of focusing on developing assets rather than income. And believe me, the older you become, the sexier your assets become!

There are many types of assets, but the main categories are:

- Businesses
- Real Estate

- Paper—Stocks, Bonds, Mutual Funds, ETFs, REITs, and so on
- Intellectual Property

Think of an asset as your employee. It becomes an economic engine that works for you twenty-four hours a day, seven days a week. As an employee, the amount of income you can make exchanging time for money is limited to how much time you can spend working; therefore, your income potential is *finite*. In contrast, the amount of income you can make from assets is *infinite*.

Businesses

When it comes to businesses, far too many people own a job instead of a business, which means they are still exchanging time for money. It is important to build your business with the right foundation, the right business systems, and the right team so that it can become an economic engine working for you. In my book *Exit Rich*, I share how to take your successful business and make it sustainable, scalable, and salable. In this book, Douglas reveals how he has successfully built businesses that work for him. By having the right teams in place, he only needs to spend six minutes a day in oversight. He has done it with several businesses and now shares how you can do the same with your business and win back your time.

Real Estate

Allow me to ask you this question: How many positive cash-flowing real estate investment properties could you own? The answer is as many as you can find, right? As a seasoned real estate investor, you will have created a successful model in selecting properties and developed a team that works alongside you (which hopefully includes a fabulous property manager). In this example, it definitely takes time to find, purchase, and rent the property up front . . . but once rented, your time is free to enjoy the fruits of your labor as you receive your rent check each month (some refer to this as mailbox money). Your team is handling the day-to-day issues that arise, which frees up your time to go find the next fabulous real estate deal! You have won your time back while owning an income-producing asset that is working for you!

Paper Assets

There are numerous ways to invest in paper assets. Unless you are a broker, day trader, or the issuer of the paper, investments in paper assets are generally considered passive investments. Similar to real estate, you spend time analyzing and determining what you want to invest in and then it works for you. Financial planners will recommend that you diversify across paper asset categories.

In contrast, I recommend that you diversify across all asset categories—businesses, real estate, paper, and intellectual property. When you do this, you are best prepared to minimize the impact from downturns in the market.

Intellectual Property

When you share your brilliance with the world through the written word, an oral or video presentation, or through an invention where you solve a problem or serve a need, you create an intellectual property asset. Your brand, logo, database, and business systems are all intellectual property. The term *goodwill* when a business sells generally represents the value from intangible assets like intellectual property. Too few business owners take the time to identify these valuable intellectual property assets. Even fewer protect and then leverage them through systems that turn the intellectual property into income-producing assets.

All of these asset categories can work together to create financial independence for you and your family. In *The 6-Minute Work Day*, Douglas explains how these types of assets help you gain your freedom.

To accomplish this, Douglas adds another very important category to his list of assets: networks.

Networks

He shares: "The highest value skill in building your business, wealth, financial and time freedom, and everything else you want is to learn how to build and maintain high-level relationships. You'll soon find that your success in business really comes down to relationships. The most successful entrepreneurs in the world know how to assemble the best individuals and get them to work collaboratively to create outcomes that would be impossible otherwise."

I wholeheartedly agree with this. I teach the Power of Association in my book *Three Feet from Gold: Turn Your Obstacles into Opportunities*. I also share the Personal Success Equation:

$$[(P + T) \times A \times A] + F$$
$$[(Passion + Talent)] \times Association \times Action] + Faith$$

Your passion and talent are all about you! Your passion combined with your education and experience creates your "why." Most of us stop there and believe we have to do everything on our own. True success comes from the Power of Association—having the right mentor and the right people on your team. People who are strong where you are weak. Combine the right associations with taking action and you speed your way to winning back your time. But the last element, faith, is very important—faith in what you are doing, faith that it is needed and necessary, and faith that you will succeed. As a very important side note, when I mentor people, it is usually the area of association and faith where they need the most help. And those two areas go hand in hand. When you have the right people around you, they will keep you going even when you are having a bad day, thus strengthening your faith.

Please review this formula as it pertains to your own personal success. I provide a guide at www.personalsuccess equation.com that may help you discover opportunities for immediate action to speed your path in winning back your time.

Doing Better Instead of Doing More

Hand in hand with having the right associations, you must be intentional with how you invest your time. Douglas shares the very important concept of "doing better instead of doing more." The hundreds of successful businesspeople he interviewed were very consistent in how they *invested* their time.

"They actually flipped the funnel upside down and did less. Maybe *less* isn't the best word to choose. Let me rephrase that. They did better. They were more selective about where they spent their time. They put their time into things they had thought carefully about and prepared for. They did not meet with everyone. Again, they selected carefully those they would give their time to and they made sure there was purpose and preparation in every meeting. They also did broadcast their message to everyone; they delivered a careful and calculated message to the segments that were most likely to respond."

This is just a snapshot of the incredible wisdom that Douglas shares in *The 6-Minute Work Day*. I am honored to write the foreword, but even more thrilled to learn from him. I have implemented some of his strategies already in my businesses and I invite you to do so as well.

To your success!

—**Sharon Lechter, CGMA**
Author of *Think and Grow Rich for Women*
Coauthor of *Exit Rich*, *Three Feet from Gold*, *Outwitting the Devil*, *Rich Dad Poor Dad*, and fourteen other books in the Rich Dad series
www.sharonlechter.com

INTRODUCTION

Today has been a highly profitable and productive day.

My company had just over three hundred new clients purchase from us. We built out the platform to launch three new products over the next several weeks. We hired seven new employees and started their training. We completed a licensing deal to have my intellectual property translated into Mandarin Chinese and Japanese. We finalized a partnership with one of our competitors to create a powerful collaboration. And we started a significant review of a handful of other opportunities—some of which we will commit to and a handful of others we may reserve for a future time.

This is a typical day.

When I tell people about how busy I am, they often start by asking how I have time for a life. They often ask: "What time did you get up? How late did you work? When did you see your family? Do you ever get to see your family? Where do you find the time?" They speculate that I must be one of the most unbalanced people they've ever met.

My favorite part is when I get to see the look on their faces when I tell them that, on average, I actually work only about six minutes each day.

"Six minutes, that's all." As I reveal this, I often get a number of responses. Most of them are disbelief. When they confirm to make sure they've heard me right, they often bring up the various successes they have observed and point out that my companies have customers on several continents, operate in multiple languages, manage and control several million dollars in assets, and have teams, employees, and operations working nearly every day of the year. They don't believe fitting all that into six minutes per day is possible. Some have even told me my watch must be broken.

I generally confess that my early days did not start out lasting six minutes. And even now there are exceptions when I spend more time working. But the reality is, yes, I generally work six minutes a day.

In this book I am going to unfold how this is possible and how you can do the same.

I want to start by getting clear on what this book is and what it is not. This is not a get-rich-quick or get-rich-easy book. In fact, this book has very little to do with money. What this book is primarily about is systems and leadership. I am not talking about bossing people around and getting them to do all the work for you while you go on holiday. That kind of strategy may work in the short term, but very quickly those engaged in helping you will lose momentum, motivation, and vision. You'll soon see as you follow me through the lessons in this book that there is a way to get organized in such a manner that you can have what you want, for yourself and those you work with, and still keep your time.

THE IMPORTANCE OF TIME

There are a lot of things that are being taught right now that you will need to let go of. Some of these I will share as we go through the book, but there is one idea you've probably heard before that I want to get rid of right now:

The wealthy do not trade time for money.

You've heard this, right?

You might even tell yourself that you agree with the idea. Lots of entrepreneurs and business owners say this, but then right away they get back to work. You even see many of the popular business "gurus" online preaching the idea that if you want to create success you need to learn how to hustle, grind, wake up early (they call it the 5:00 a.m. club), or be prepared to work into the wee hours of the night.

They try to drill this idea of hard work and lengthy hours into everyone they talk to. There are a few problems with this idea of hustling and grinding. The first is that it is in direct opposition to the concept that "the wealthy do not trade time for money." This notion of work is an *invitation* to pursue the path of trading time for money. The other thing I find incredibly suspect is that while these "gurus" are continually promoting the hustle and grind, I haven't yet heard any of them clarify what you should be doing during that time. To me it looks like they really don't have an answer. It's easier to say get to work than it is to say what you should be working on. They don't really know.

It's almost like they are saying if you want to get somewhere, you need to start running. Don't you think it might be better to know where you are going first? That's one of the big questions we are going to answer in this book. In addition to helping you clarify the final destination, together we'll unfold the map and chart the shortcuts.

The notion that success must be achieved through grind and hustle is a lie made up by those who don't have real answers to get you to where you want to go.

Now, you may be wondering how I could possibly think I have any answers for you. What could possibly qualify me to say that what you have heard from others will not work?

Let me share a bit of my journey and you can then decide if there is any merit to what you are about to learn.

I did not come from a wealthy family. I was not given a ton of money as an inheritance to buy my way to a life of freedom and luxury. In fact, I was raised in a lower-income home. My father worked in construction and my mother babysat kids in our home. I wore hand-me-down clothes into high school. We were broke.

I learned my life lessons in this environment.

To make the money my family needed, my father worked overtime and my mother babysat more kids. To pay for a family vacation, we would take on family projects on which we would work together.

The equation was: if you want more, you need to work more. But what I found is that no matter how much work we put in, there was always more to do to get what we needed.

When I went into the work world, the only expectation I had was that I would gain financial freedom by putting in more hours. Perhaps some of you reading can relate? Maybe you were raised in a home like mine. If you were, you also know that, in the end, no matter how hard you worked or how many hours you put in, you didn't seem to get ahead.

To build a six-minute workday, you first need to consider your upbringing:

- What ideas around money were you raised with?
- How do you believe your financial freedom could arrive?

Many believe you can't have financial freedom unless you earn it through significant hard work and sacrifice. There is a principle in psychology known as investment bias that suggests people often self-sabotage if they think that success or rewards come too easily. Investment bias leaves an individual feeling like they are not worthy to receive a reward unless they have paid a significant price. The reality is that there need not be a trade of time for money in the ways that so many of us have come to believe.

There may not be a trade, but there is a formula.

Needless to say, as I entered the work world, I was ready to work hard. I decided to take a summer job selling pest control in California while I was in college. Each day in the summer heat, I went door-to-door and tried to convince people to purchase a pest control contract. My supervisors promised me success if I put in more hours and worked harder. But as you can predict, the hours I was putting in started eating up other areas of my life. There was no way I could keep it up.

But I was desperate. This job was my hope to return to college. I needed the money. So I kept putting in all the hours I could in hopes that the money would come.

Without sounding too dramatic, I began to lose hope. I felt like I was spinning my wheels and getting nowhere fast.

I have talked with other entrepreneurs around the globe, and they all had moments like this. They've experienced giving everything they could without getting the results they needed. Sometimes, that's the moment when they quit or assume that they are on the wrong path and choose something else. In fact, many of those who've been fooled by the invitation to hustle, grind, wake up early, and stay up late generally run into a state of burnout. I get it. That's kind of where I was.

And although this wasn't my own company, it was similar to others who do own their own companies. If you are stuck in this kind of a trade, you are literally an employee, not a business owner. We will definitely get into this lie and illusion further in the book.

So, what happened next not only changed my life, but eventually led to me helping to change the lives of hundreds of business owners and entrepreneurs worldwide.

LEARNING FROM OTHERS TO WORK SMARTER, NOT HARDER

I met with a mentor of mine one afternoon and he gave me two books with an invitation to start working smarter, not harder. After I learned about this concept, I started hearing about it everywhere. I soon found that although there were lots of people talking about it, most people didn't really know how to do it.

The authors of these books shared the stories of individuals who had achieved massive success—people like Henry Ford, John Rockefeller, Andrew Carnegie, J. Paul Getty, and other extremely wealthy people of that era. Missing from these stories were lessons about working smarter that I could apply to my own life. To me, these were a bunch of old people who had nothing in common with me. Their strategies were so far distant from my experience that they had little meaning.

Then I had the big aha moment. I thought: If someone were to profile today's business titans, who would be the case studies of massive success? Perhaps these would be the people who could unfold how to effectively create freedom in terms of both finance and time. I was disappointed to find that no one had compiled lessons like these from contemporary business leaders and I realized that if I was going to learn how to work smarter, I would need to start learning directly from those who were doing it.

With my new mission to learn firsthand from the world's top businesspeople in my own day, I started meeting successful businesspeople wherever I could find them. At first, I started locally with those in my community. I took every millionaire who would meet with me to lunch. For the course of about a year and half, I had meetings several times a week.

My mind was expanding in incredible ways. My complete perspective was shifting away from the idea that money and time were connected. They are not. Soon, I was talking with higher and higher levels of business titans because once the leaders I was meeting understood my mission, they volunteered their help and made introductions.

Over the next decade, I met more than four hundred of the world's top business leaders and entrepreneurs. Theirs is the expertise you are going to get in this book.

I am going to share with you what I learned as I sat face-to-face with the founders of companies like Reebok, FedEx, Ted Baker, UGG boots, and others.

I will share with you what the CEOs of Southwest Airlines, Fruit of the Loom, Nike, KFC, and others taught me about managing people, projects, and profits.

I will share with you what team leaders for companies like Uber, Philip Morris, Purina, Toyota, and others taught me about building systems, marketing, and positioning.

And perhaps most importantly, I will share what I learned about how to get organized in the most effective ways to not only gain market share but keep your life in the process.

YOUR BUSINESS BEGINNINGS MATTER

During my time of meeting with the top business leaders, I got bit by the business bug. In other words, as I met with these multimillionaire and billionaire business leaders, I decided that my success would come if I started a business. I had a really good idea for a company and all my planning seemed sound.

I decided the next best step I could do was meet with one of my business-leader friends to get some advice on how I would launch this enterprise and build it into a huge empire.

I still remember meeting my friend for lunch at a high-end restaurant in downtown Vancouver, Canada. Under one arm I carried what I thought was the most impressive business plan ever created. As I pulled up a chair, I began to unfold my business idea. At first, he seemed quite impressed. My confidence was soaring.

I decided it was time to shift into my questions:

- "How can I find my customers?"
- "What's the best way for me to market?"
- "How can I find a way to distribute these products?"
- "How will I scale into other territories?"
- "How can I deal with competitors?"
- "What should I do to get some financing?"

Perhaps these are some of the same questions you have thought about as you've looked at starting a company. I thought they were great questions. But as I asked them, my friend smiled and simply said, "I can tell you're going to start a small company."

I was surprised and hurt at the same time. What did he mean, a small company? I was not on a mission to start a small company. In fact, I have never yet met an entrepreneur who told me he had only a small, reserved vision of what was to come. All of the entrepreneurs that I have met are visionaries and they want to create something with impact. Something that rises high and reaches far.

I asked him to clarify what he meant.

He repeated, "I can tell, you're going to start a small company."

I still didn't get it. I decided not to jump to conclusions. I had learned so much from similar conversations so I decided to hold back judgment and consider what I might be missing. I asked him to explain.

He did. Pay careful attention—this insight will be the beginning of your six-minute workday.

He told me that in regard to my company I was asking selfish questions. He then pointed out that all my questions involved just me. "What could *I*?" "How should *I*?" "Where will *I*?" Those are selfish questions.

They are limiting. You can never create great success or scale while asking them. In fact, if you look at most struggling business owners, not only do they assign themselves all of these questions but they get to work guarding the responsibility for the answers. They feel that everything is their duty because they are the business owner. As a result, they limit their success.

My multimillionaire friend continued to explain that if I wanted to create a thriving, expansive business then I needed to ask more empowering questions that invited the participation of others. He rephrased my questions in this way:

- "Who can help me find more customers?"
- "Who knows the best ways for me to market?"
- "Who can help me find ways to distribute these products?"
- "Who can help me scale into other territories?"

- "Who can help me work with my competitors?" (More on this later.)
- "Who can help me acquire financing?"

When we shift from being a solopreneur or a self-employed person and recognize that a true entrepreneur isn't the one that does all the work, we begin to create something of significance. The word *entrepreneur* is very misunderstood; it is actually closer in meaning to the description of a conductor in an orchestra. The most successful entrepreneurs in the world know how to assemble the best individuals and get them to work collaboratively to create outcomes that would be impossible otherwise.

As an entrepreneur, your job is not to have all the answers, but rather to hire and find people and resources that can help you find the best answers—and as you discover those answers, you become the conductor and put your people and resources into their best places. The most powerful thing you can be is teachable.

You are trying to create a powerful and thrilling symphony—one in which everyone involved gets to enjoy the music. When you build it correctly, your customers love it! Your employees and support teams enjoy it! Your family enjoys it! And, most of all, you get to enjoy it!

I love what Steve Jobs once said about teams like this: "We don't hire smart people and tell them what to do. We hire smart people so they can tell us what to do."

You'll find that your most important mission in building your six-minute workday starts with finding those smart people. Nurturing these types of relationships is the highest-value skill you could ever develop.

The pages ahead offer you actionable insights for building a strong symphony for your business from the very beginning to ensure all systems hum harmoniously even as you transition to a six-minute workday and, in fact, make that dream workday a reality.

My goal with this book is to help you create a prosperous and balanced life. Whether you are an entrepreneur or someone who just wants to be more effective in your work, you will find helpful strategies in this book. You will quickly see that so many of the lessons you need to thrive in any economy are much easier and more straightforward than so many others are making them seem.

Part 1

BUILDING YOUR
BUSINESS

| | | | |

Chapter 1

WHY A WORKDAY?

Have you ever thought about why we have a "workday"? What is the purpose it serves? How did it get created and, most importantly, why do we build our lives around it?

The reality is that most people don't think enough about these questions. Most people just accept the workday structure as the way of life.

One of the first things I want to emphatically state is that you do have a choice. Your life doesn't have to be constructed around the idea of working nine to five, or more.

The workday is an old-fashioned idea.

Most people go to work to make the money needed to survive. But if you look closely, the workday is the foundational concept of trading time for money. To survive, we have been taught that we need to commit to a forty-hour workweek. In addition—and this is the dreadful part—you need to be prepared to spend most of your life doing it.

Isn't that an interesting word we use? *Spend* your time, *spend* your week, *spend* your life. One shift I would like you to start considering is changing that word *spend* to *invest*. Spending often doesn't improve your situation, while investing is calculated to do so. We will talk more about this concept after we lay a little bit more foundational work so you can recognize what counts as a good investment of your effort and time, because not all activity is created equal. Write that part down now.

One of the reasons so many people are caught in the workday trap is that they really don't understand the idea of financial freedom and how it works. Let's take a minute and clarify this concept using a quick exercise.

With a piece of paper in front of you, take a moment and consider what financial freedom looks like to you. Write down the ideas that come into your mind when you hear the term *financial freedom*. Add everything to the list that you feel needs to be mentioned. Make notes for about a minute and then start reading again. Now take a careful look at your answers. If you are like most people I have done this exercise with, you will have mentioned that to you financial freedom means things like:

- Being able to choose what you will do every day
- Being able to travel

- Having the cars and clothing you want
- Spending time with people you choose
- Giving back to your community
- Being totally debt free
- Paying off your house
- Spending more time with family
- Having a ton of money in your bank account
- Never having to worry about money
- Buying anything you want

These are all typical answers to this question of what financial freedom means. But they are also exactly the answers that keep people from ever attaining true financial freedom. Here's the lesson: These descriptions are all descriptions of events. Even though some of these desires are noble, emotionally satisfying, and worthy goals, they are not the correct definition of financial freedom.

Your financial freedom is not an emotional experience.

Financial freedom is actually a specific number, and it's much easier to attain than you might think. Let me illustrate. To determine your financial freedom number, you must take a look at your expenses. For most people, their bills arrive in a thirty-day cycle. Let's take a look at an example of bills from the last thirty days. (The numbers I am using are for example purposes only. This is not a complete list of acceptable monthly expenses. Your list will have some of the same things and perhaps many things that are not listed here. The things on this list might be higher or lower than what you are experiencing. To be accurate in finding your own financial freedom number, you will have to build your own sheet. You can download the worksheet to help you do this exercise for your own expenses for free at www.SixMinuteWorkday.com.)

Mortgage	$1,200
Utilities	$350
Car payment	$550
Insurance	$200
Gas (for car)	$80
Groceries	$300
Internet	$120
TV/Cable	$100
Total Monthly Expenses	$2,900

With these monthly expenses, you must generate $2,900 per month to meet all of your obligations. This total is the financial freedom number. While this isn't the book to talk about passive income, I want to point out that knowing your financial freedom number gives you power. The more you understand how to create income to offset your monthly expenses that are not attached to your workday, you no longer need the workday. This is a primary principle in constructing your six-minute workday and establishing financial freedom.

Once you determine your financial freedom number, the question then becomes about how you can generate income outside of a workday obligation.

Terri is one of my students in the UK. When we first met, her finances were a mess. She had a strong entrepreneurial spirit but with each venture she began she found herself upside down because she didn't recognize where she was or where she was headed. Her idea of financial freedom for her and her family was all experiential. She didn't have any way to measure if she was making progress or not. Once she understood that financial freedom was an actual number she could work toward, things changed for her. She has been able to build her life and business in such a way that she is now closing the gap between where she is and where she wants to be. Financial freedom and abundance is now within her grasp.

Tyler in Las Vegas, Nevada, was experiencing a similar problem. Money was coming in and going out. Lots of it. But he was still always broke. He had several entrepreneurial ventures going on at once but he was always trying to figure out the money part. After learning about getting specific and clear with his numbers and setting some measurable goals around his financial abundance, he began to be more careful about where the money was going each month. Within a

*short amount of time, he made some personal commitments,
which allowed him to shift toward the path of a six-minute
workday and an annual income of $350,000 plus investments
to satisfy his financial freedom in the future.*

My goal, as I share in my trainings, is not for you to be
financially free. I want you to be financially abundant. Freedom by itself means that you have your obligations covered.
I want you to be abundant insomuch that you have the financial means to do everything your heart desires. In fact, I'd be
willing to venture a guess that those of you who are entrepreneurs chose this path because this kind of financial expression was what you had in mind.

I should also point out that financial freedom and abundance apply not just to your personal life, but also your business life. You should take the time to outline your monthly
business expenses and start to build a plan around how
these obligations can be met without the direct attachment
to your business activities. During the 2020 pandemic, we
saw many businesses simply die off because their revenues
were attached to the activities of their customers. When the
customers could not buy from them because of the lock-
down and other limitations, their income sources disappeared. While we don't have the scope in this book to talk
about this in great depth, one of the best lessons I was given
by my business mentors was to use a portion of your business income to build the financial freedom of your business

by diversifying or investing in other cashflow opportunities for your business.

To clarify these principles and how you are going to get to financial freedom and then financial abundance in both your personal life and your business life, you will need to understand the following four positions:

- Financial Insecurity
- Financial Security
- Financial Freedom
- Financial Abundance

We've already talked about the last two—financial freedom and financial abundance. I'll come back to those again in a second. But the first two—financial insecurity and financial security—are really what keep people stuck in the workday.

By definition, financial insecurity is a description of people who are working hard to make a living but, even though they are trading a forty-hour workweek or more, they are not bringing home enough money to meet their needs. To survive they often have to skip paying bills or put them off until they come up with some more money. Obviously, they are in a difficult and stressful situation. They have only a few options. They have to learn to make some sacrifices and spend less than they make. This is not always easy. I recently read a breakdown of the expenses of the average single parent. Sometimes the

sacrifices they might have to make could include food, hous-
ing, and other necessities. This is an extremely hard place to
be. The alternative option to making these sacrifices is to find
additional income sources. For most individuals experiencing
financial insecurity, the only thing they understand is what I
previously understood, and that is: if you want more money,
you need to work more hours.

The next level up is known as financial security, but it's
not really a step up in your financial life. It basically means
that your paycheck covers your bills; you are earning enough
money to meet your obligations. But the reality is that you are
just one unexpected bill away from trouble. If you have the
brakes go out on your car, or your kid needs braces, or you
have an unexpected medical expense, you risk dropping right
back into financial insecurity.

The scary thing about financial security or the paycheck-
to-paycheck situation is that so many people are in it. CNBC
reported on December 11, 2020, that 63 percent of all Amer-
icans are in this situation. They also pointed out that since
the start of the COVID-19 pandemic, the number has been
steadily increasing.

Many businesses are following exactly the same trend.
Prior to the pandemic they were already operating on thin
margins. When there were customers they seemed to do okay,
but if something didn't work out right or a particular client
disappeared or a deal fell through, they were in trouble and
went right back to financial insecurity.

There are ways to structure things for greater safety in both your business and personal life.

Your goal as a business owner is really the final category of financial abundance. This is really the one that everyone should also strive for in their personal life as well. Too many people are focused on balancing their checkbook, when the real goal should be to get way out of balance on the abundance side of things. Balance is a tightrope walk that is always on the suspenseful verge of challenge and disaster. I want you to be so unbalanced toward abundance that your fears and concerns disappear.

One of the most important things that many people forget when it comes to financial abundance is to approach it as an actual number. It's not just about creating experiences. You have to know what it looks like so you can determine how close or far you are to reaching it. Naturally, as you reach one goal, you can always increase the number to reflect your current priorities.

I am a strong advocate that you should also deeply consider why you have chosen these numbers. The stronger your why-power, the stronger your will-power.

Vision boards have been quite popular in recent years. A vision board, sometimes called a dream board, is generally a place where people share pictures or images of the things that they want most in their life. While I think these are great tools, I believe that most people have been creating them in an incomplete way. Your vision board shouldn't stop at pictures. It should also include a description of what something costs—a goal that is specific and clear is attainable and near. Your financial abundance can be attained only if you put a number on it.

A few years ago, I decided I wanted a Ferrari. Lots of people say that they want one. You might even want one. The reality is, most people stop there. I decided if I really wanted a Ferrari, I needed to follow my own advice and get specific. I started doing some research, and the first thing I clarified was the model. I decided I wanted a 360 Modena Spider. I knew it needed to be a convertible. I was flexible on the color, but I thought either a blue or a yellow would be perfect. I put the description, including the current retail price, on my vision board. I also added a few reasons why I want *this* car and not just any car. I was very specific.

Naturally, by being so clear and precise, my attention was now directed to this car when references to it appeared in my life. People who knew that I was looking also brought information and opportunities to me from time to time. And one day a car that fit my vision perfectly came into my life in a way that was accessible.

Because I had taken the time to learn all I could about the car in advance, I was prepared when it arrived. I was even able to recognize that what this seller was asking for it was a really good deal. Naturally, I bought it. It was a fun car.

I want you to think of the important takeaways here, because these lessons will be important for us to consider in the next chapters. There was more time spent planning for the Ferrari than purchasing it. By the time the car had arrived, I had done all my homework to determine if it was a good deal and a right fit for me. I was ready in advance and so I was able to receive the car.

Travis lives in Edmonton, Canada. He had been using his vision board as his primary resource for recording his goals for years. When we met, he expressed that while he enjoyed having a vision board it didn't really seem to make any impact in his life. I challenged him to add more specific details to his vision board, and when he did, they really made a difference for him. He now drives the exact car featured on his vision board and coincidentally married a woman who looks very much like the picture of the woman he also posted there.

In addition to financial freedom and abundance being about money, I would invite you to include two additional freedoms: time and location. These are often manifestations of having gotten your financial life figured out. Certainly, these two freedoms cannot exist in the traditional workday.

When you have your financial freedom (Freedom #1: Money) and abundance flowing, your time begins to return to you (Freedom #2: Time). How do you get to have your money and your time? Some gurus are quick to say that you can have both—have your cake and eat it too. They're right, but they are leaving out something. It isn't automatic. You have to invest time in laying the groundwork for obtaining both. You have to prepare and bake the cake before you can enjoy it. We'll be spending a lot of effort in the upcoming chapters sharing the recipe and expectations around doing just that.

I believe that most often location freedom (Freedom #3) follows the achievements of both Freedoms #1 and #2. But I have seen many instances where this freedom has actually jumped right into the number one spot and has facilitated the other two freedoms. So, if you obtain these freedoms in a different order, that's all right. With the ever-increasing developments in technology, you can do business from anywhere in the world and with anyone in the world. There are no longer limits on where you can live and work.

Return to the list of monthly expenses you used to calculate your financial freedom number. You'll be pleased to know that just changing location can diminish these expenses dramatically. Tim Ferriss in his book *The 4-Hour Workweek* points out that the living expenses in many parts of the world are drastically lower than those in America or Europe.

About two years ago, I decided to agree to a speaking tour that included the Philippines, Kuala Lumpur, Bali, Thailand, and Singapore. While I had visited Asia several times before, I had never lived or traveled there for an extended period of time. I was at times very surprised how inexpensive daily living was. For example, I remember seeing a movie and paying only $1.25, which included all the concessions I could carry. Each morning I would have an amazing full breakfast and it cost less than $2. I stayed in a five-star hotel at a rate of only $25 per night. In another location, I rented a two-bedroom apartment with a big office, far more space than I would ever need considering I was by myself, but it cost only $60 for the week. The roof had the most incredible infinity pool with a view of the nearby ocean.

One of my favorite experiences was during my first visit to Bali. I stopped in the lobby of my hotel and started looking at the tourist brochures. The girl behind the counter saw me looking and asked if I wanted to see some of the things featured in them. I shrugged and said, "Maybe later, we'll see." I didn't say it as a commitment, just a passing thought. I soon left the hotel lobby and walked down the street to see the neighborhood. About ten minutes later, my cell phone rang. It was the girl from the hotel. She simply said, "Your driver is here."

I didn't understand exactly what was happening and I thought perhaps some of the others whom I was traveling with had arranged something, so I came back to the hotel. When I got there, I found she had found a driver to take me to all of the tourist locations I wanted to see. He would drive me to each one and wait for me as my personal chauffeur wherever I wanted to go. He would be with me for as long as I wanted over the next two days. The total cost for his services? Twenty dollars.

Location freedom can make a difference. Location freedom isn't just about the money, however. Naturally, as you read of these experiences, you may have thought about some of the cool things I was able to enjoy while I was in Asia. I was able to ride elephants and visit a Buddhist temple (and get blessed by a Buddhist monk). I was able to visit a wood-carving facility. I was able to see where and how they made coffee in Bali. I was able to visit spectacular waterfalls and beaches, and several ancient shrines. It was an incredible experience. Visiting these locations was exciting and expanded my horizons.

I have been blessed to have these kinds of experiences in many other countries and locations around the world. Location freedom in my opinion can be one of the most fulfilling freedoms that exists.

Just as with financial abundance, I think it is a great idea to describe with clarity some of the things you would like to do or see in your life. Remember that a goal that is specific and clear becomes attainable and near.

I do want to recognize that perhaps not everyone reading this book is ready to leave their family and friends for a life of travel. That's okay. I have a number of students who have embraced the remote laptop lifestyle part of the six-minute workday. They spend their full six minutes working and then head off snorkeling or sightseeing. Some have even taken their entire family with them. However, more often than not, they choose to spend their location freedom right in their own community. They spend more time doing what they want with whomever they want.

Most of the time, this is me. After my six-minute workday, you'll usually find me picking up my kids from school, riding

Exercise

Take some time to do some evaluating and planning for your personal life and business. Determine your financial freedom number and your current income. Look at the difference between the two numbers and get clarity about how you are going to get to financial freedom. This clarity is going to come in handy as we proceed through the next steps of building your six-minute workday in the upcoming chapters.

bikes with the kids, playing at the park, watching movies with the family, or just hanging out. One of my biggest hobbies is practicing Brazilian jiujitsu. I train almost every day. Not just because I love it, but because I have structured my life to give me freedom.

Your choices will be different from mine or those of others whom I have taught. The most important thing is that you will have choices. Choice is the most wonderful gift you can ever create. I hope you will use it wisely.

QUESTIONS: WHY A WORKDAY?

Reflect on where you currently are in your journey to financial abundance by considering the following questions:

- Where did your concept of the workday come from?
- How much of your life are you trading to meet your obligations?
- What is your financial freedom number?
- What does financial abundance look like for you and your company?
- Do you use vision boards? If so, how specific are you in outlining your goals and desires?
- Are there other geographical locations that might help you gain financial freedom or lifestyle freedom?
- Are there places you would like to see and/or things you would like to do that only financial freedom can enable?

ACTION STEPS

1. Take a careful look at your current sources of income. Where is your income coming from, and what are you trading for that income? Can you identify a better trade, such as trading expensive rent for a lower financial freedom number?

2. Get specific about what you want in terms of finances, location, and experiences. The more specific you can be, the more likely it will be that you can reach those goals. In future chapters we'll discuss how to involve others to help you to achieve what's on your vision

board. But others can only help you if you can clearly explain what you're striving for.

3. Decide now that part of your resources will be given as a contribution to help others. Remember that helping others with our time, talents, resources, and money is one of the greatest sources of joy. If you're a business owner, I also invite you to elect a charity of your choice that will be supported through your entrepreneurial efforts. Not only will you be a crusader for doing good in the world but you will attract better things into your life and business. If you don't currently have a cause in mind, head over to www.EazyDonate.com and partner with us on some of the fantastic causes we have chosen to support.

CHAPTER AHA MOMENTS

- The workday is an extension of the trade of time for money.
- Not all activities are created equal.
- When you know your financial freedom number, you have power.
- Financial abundance is the goal; it is also a number.
- When you are specific and clear, you dramatically increase the chances of your success.
- Helping others is the source of your greatest joy.

Chapter 2

WHAT CAN BE DONE IN SIX MINUTES?

A t first glance, six minutes doesn't seem like a long time. Six minutes is literally only 360 seconds. Most people dismiss the idea that anything great could be accomplished let alone expected as a result of six minutes. There are many people who said to me (even on live TV) that they don't believe I can manage or run multiple million-dollar companies in only six minutes per day.

The reality is that there are some days that I do spend a little longer than six minutes working. (Especially if I chose to take a teaching or speaking assignment. But those activities are actually separate from the management of my companies and wealth.) Realistically, however, most days I am spending six minutes or less.

There are countless examples of powerful results being created in very concise moments of time.

When I was conducting my interviews with the world's top business leaders, I had a singular experience that taught me about the ideas we have about time spent working and how they stand in the way of financial abundance.

I reached out to a business owner I wanted to interview. He had done some amazing things, including building his business from a concept to a multimillion-dollar venture and doing business in several countries. I knew there was a lot I could learn from him. (Coincidentally, it wasn't always the biggest or most well-known companies that taught me the most. This was one such experience.)

As I got through to him on the telephone, I simply asked if I could meet with him for fifteen minutes for some questions. He agreed and we set a date and location. I was excited and arrived with my prepared questions.

After I shook his hand, I was surprised to see him reach into his pocket, pull out a stopwatch, and set it on the table. "You've got fifteen minutes," he said. "Let's get started."

This was the first time I'd ever witnessed someone demonstrate how strict they were with their time. I remember being extremely grateful that I was thoroughly prepared with my questions. Thank goodness we finished that day within the allotted time. As we shook hands and I got ready to leave, I told him I was very intrigued by the concept of the stopwatch and asked if I could meet him again to discuss it. He agreed for an additional fifteen minutes another day.

As we parted ways, the idea of the stopwatch lingered with me. I had so many questions about why he felt it was important. What inspired him to start using it? What value had it created in his life? Was this something I should start doing in my life?

When I met with him the second time, I jumped directly into my questions about the stopwatch.

As I did, he started by saying that I had passed the test. He explained that most people don't take time seriously, but when I came prepared and could accomplish everything that I set out to do in the fifteen minutes I had, he knew I understood the power of preparation and using time wisely.

He then began to explain that so many people feel that every meeting must take an hour, noting that this is a leftover from our time in school. We were taught that a math class, or social studies, or science, or whatever subject, fit best in a one-hour class period and so we have it in our minds that every meeting going forward should be turned into a one-hour session.

Since then, I have also observed how many times people want to meet with me and make it a one-hour thing. They ask to meet me at a Starbucks or wherever and spend the first thirty minutes talking about fluff and things that have no relevance to the reason we are meeting. Now, don't get me wrong,

I'm not saying that your meetings need to be sharp and without connection or emotion, but the reality is that most meetings are a complete waste of time.

My stopwatch-wielding mentor pointed out that when people know that time is short, they always come better prepared. He then shared a saying that I have since adopted in everything I do: "You teach people how to treat you." I have found this idea to be incredibly true in life and business. You teach people how to treat time when they are with you based on how they observe you treat time.

I haven't always practiced what I have preached, but I didn't understand until after I had made the mistake. Here is one of those moments.

As a young man, one of the first companies I started launched just as the internet was coming out. I opened up an online directory to support the film industry. Actors and actresses could post their headshots and resumes with us and casting directors would then use our site to find talent. I called the company casting-call.net. Pretty simple, right? (It's gone now, so you won't find it today. This was in the late 1990s and I later sold the company.)

In those days we actually had physical offices. I had offices in major cities in Canada and the US. I got pretty organized so I didn't have to go into the office that often. I had teams of people that would meet with talent and coordinate our efforts. Most of the time when I would come in, I obeyed my own rules of professionalism. I would even show up in a suit.

But one day, I came in much more relaxed, wearing shorts and a T-shirt. As I was in the office that day, I took a much more casual approach. I sat around chatting up the team more like a friend than the director of the team. This went on for the entire afternoon. I forgot I was the leader and fell into the friend zone. As I left, I knew in the back of my mind I had made a mistake. However, I did not learn. I did the same thing the next week. Employees began to joke around with me as they would a buddy. And although that felt fun, I began to wonder if I was setting myself up for problems. Sure enough, the problems came.

For the next month, reports I requested from this office were more casual. I called one day and found that they had all decided to have a short day and leave early because it was nice and sunny outside. One of my team members started dating actresses that came into the office. (We had a policy against this.) And I had to terminate one of these team members for "borrowing" some money. I had never had these problems when I was running a tighter ship with higher standards.

Do yourself a favor and separate your intimate friends from your business relationships. I'm not saying don't be courteous. I am saying don't be casual. This all begins with how you choose to demonstrate how you value time.

Becky attended one of my events in London. She had been trying to be buddies with the people that worked for her and it seemed to be creating the same casual atmosphere I spoke about above. She was seriously stressed about it as these were good people she didn't want to fire. And when she tried to encourage them to step up to a more professional self, they didn't take her seriously. She decided to start stepping up herself and become a living example of what she was trying to create. In the end, one of the people she had on the team actually left thinking things were getting too serious but everyone else stepped up to the higher standard and the profits of the company tripled.

A LOT CAN BE DONE IN A SHORT PERIOD OF TIME

An activity will generally expand to the amount of time you allow for it. The opposite is also true. An activity can be done much faster if there isn't a lot of time available for it to be accomplished.

Perhaps you've had an experience like the one I had in high school. Our teacher began the semester by announcing that at the end of the term there would be an assignment due. We could work on it all semester and could even submit it early if we liked. Naturally, because the assignment was due at the end of the semester, I thought to myself, as did most of the other students, that I had lots of time. There was no need to worry about it now because the deadline was so far in the distance; I would get around to it.

As you can guess, the time passed quickly and I hadn't really done any work for this assignment. Suddenly, the last week arrived and I was forced to confront the looming deadline.

Just as you have probably done in similar situations, I put myself into high gear and literally in one evening I was able to complete most of the assignment. And within another night or so, I was finished. A project that was supposed to take a semester took only a handful of hours.

The same is true of nearly everything in our life. If we get focused and get to work in a concentrated burst, we can often do far more than we expect. The task we have to do will always expand or shrink to the amount of time we decide it needs.

Start looking at your tasks in more productive shorter bursts of time and you'll see that you can do a significant amount of work in almost no time at all.

As I began to demonstrate that I valued my time in my business relationships, those whom I worked with started showing up more prepared. Reports I received were prompt and more complete. People even started asking me what was most important in our time together. And, as you might guess, people are now rarely late, and most often early, when they meet with me.

Since having the stopwatch experience, I have begun to think differently about productivity and how I approach many aspects of my business. Understanding the value of time has also made many errors committed by less experienced busi-nesspeople glaringly clear.

The reality is, as we've discussed, that profit is not built by trading time for money. You need to make a decision now that you will not waste time in the pursuit of money. Understand-ing both time and money is essential for building an effective business while retaining your freedom and maintaining a bal-anced life.

Over the years, I have continued to meet other successful entrepreneurs, but I have also met many whom I would con-sider to be less effective. Some of them were very wealthy and had massive international brands that are highly visible and rec-ognized. But they were less effective because they worked too hard. They did not use time, systems, and their resources as effi-ciently as they might have. They were not as productive as the amount of time they spent working suggested they might be.

For example, I have heard many business coaches or well-meaning sales trainers share that the surest way of grow-ing your business is to do more. They say things like:

- If you want more clients, you need to meet with more prospects.
- If you want more prospects, you've got to go to more networking events.
- If you want more prospects, you need to market more.
- If you want to see bigger results, you need to put in more hours.

You can more or less use their formula for anything that you think you want to improve. Whatever you want to improve, you simply need to do more of it. They throw in phrases like, "It's a numbers game," and "Champions always do what is required and then some." All of those ideas are foolish.

The top business leaders in the world do not look for ways to meet more people, market more, or put in more hours.

Being productive doesn't mean looking for more to do; it means actually doing more. In fact, most often, productivity is about finding a way to do less and improve your results by being more effective. One way that I teach about accomplishing more by doing less in my seminars is through the funnel effect.

THE FUNNEL EFFECT

Imagine a funnel: a large, open cup on one end and a narrow spout at the bottom. Most people run their business like this funnel. They meet with anyone and everyone, always seeking more to add to this funnel. They put in hours and hours each day from early morning until late at night. They market as much as they can, everywhere they can, to everyone they can. They put as much effort as they can in a multitude of directions. In the end, their efforts trickle out the bottom of the funnel through the tiny spout and they are disappointed with the meager results.

The reality is that all of the top business leaders I learned from did something different. They actually flipped the funnel upside down, pouring in less effort that resulted in broader gains. Maybe *less* isn't the best word to choose. Let me rephrase that. They made *better* efforts. They were more selective about where they spent their time. They put their time into things they had thought carefully about and prepared for. They did not meet with everyone. Again, they selected carefully those they would give their time to and they made sure there was purpose and preparation for every meeting. An additional step they took was to deliver a careful and calculated message to the segments that were most likely to respond rather than marketing more.

Messaging is a great example of the funnel effect at work. Isn't it interesting that online and through social media we have hundreds if not thousands of people talking about the great business owner/leader/entrepreneur they are, while the real entrepreneurs are actually too busy to post on social media every ten minutes? Here's a rant for you. A true entrepreneur doesn't care whether or not they have one hundred thousand followers on Instagram. They are more interested in customers than followers. They also understand that large business (real business) is built by a team, not an individual with a profile on social media. And I know there are a lot of people that would disagree with me. But seriously, look at the numbers, folks—the percentage of influencers actually making real money by posting to their "followers" or "subscribers" is actually quite small. Unless your goal is fame instead of profits, or your business is marketing, you may want to look again at your business model if you're spending valuable time chasing social media followers. More on this in the upcoming chapters.

With your funnel inverted, you need to be looking more carefully at how you can make your efforts more productive. I don't want you to do more. I want you to be more focused and do the things you are doing better. Look at everything that can be improved and then, after you've improved it, look again. This will be a big part of enabling your six-minute workday later on.

Doing better instead of doing more requires more advanced planning and clarity about your purposes in the beginning. Most entrepreneurs struggle with this because they are often better creators than planners. In fact, some entrepreneurs declare that they are better at just making things work out as they unfold. They feel like there is a certain thrill when flying by the seat of their pants or improvising solutions as needed. I even heard one definition of an entrepreneur as someone who jumps off a building and makes an airplane on the way down. It's true that this ability to pivot is a valuable skill for an entrepreneur to have when troubles arise. Improvisation is not, however, a skill set that builds a business. It is a skill set that should be reserved for emergencies and thus, hopefully, used sparingly.

All of these ideas of doing more, giving more, meeting more people, and being in a constant state of pivot are common among struggling business owners. It's pretty clear why this approach of the constant hustle, grind, and push creates struggling rather than thriving businesses. These things are all a formula for burnout and exhaustion. There is no way a person can effectively run a company under this kind of constant pressure and struggle.

Of the four hundred top business leaders I interviewed, not one of them espoused this *do more* approach. Instead, I saw much more calculated efforts at creating profit systems that worked and supported the original goals of freedom that we talked about in the previous chapter.

I really like the idea that Stephen Covey teaches in his excellent book *The 7 Habits of Highly Effective People*. (By the way, I encourage all of my students to put that book in their must-read list of books.) Covey teaches that, "Private victories precede public victories." That is, you must learn how to manage yourself in private before you can expect big victories in public. That means that you must learn to use your time correctly on a personal level before you can experience the power of its value in your business. You must learn how to establish better productivity in your private life before you can expect the same kinds of things to happen in your business life.

It's also interesting as we consider the funnel effect to recognize that a lot of effort and time are wasted on activities that actually aren't helping the business that much. Often, I see young entrepreneurs who want to do something just for the sake of feeling busy. Sometimes these activities are not only a big waste of time but they are also counterproductive.

I am even aware of several cases of an entrepreneur doing damage to their business that was very costly to fix. Take the time to understand what you should be doing and which efforts really should be multiplied.

> *I met Ed in Toronto. He had been a small business owner for much of his adult life. Most of his ventures did all right, but he was always wondering why he couldn't get one of his ventures to be more successful. It was then that he learned about the funnel effect principle. As he looked at his efforts, he began to realize that he had put in a lot of time, but that his efforts were all about how much time he could put in rather than about how effective he was being. The next day he told me that he canceled half of his meetings and started looking more carefully at how he used his day. As he began to be more strategic, he sent me an email that confessed that with more planning he was able to get the same results in one hour that he had previously achieved in a full day of working 7:00 a.m. to 7:00 p.m. He was very excited to discover this and so was his family.*

THE DIFFERENCE BETWEEN STUPIDITY AND TENACITY

Many entrepreneurs over the years have come to me with a question: "If I do less, won't I get even worse results?" Often, this question comes from those who have been trying to get their business to work for a number of years but no matter what they do, they can't seem to get things going. When I talk about trying to do less to be more productive, they get really frustrated and point out that even the results they are creating now barely keep them profitable.

In some circumstances these frustrated and struggling entrepreneurs have asked if they should just throw in the towel. Inevitably they tell me the story from Napoleon Hill's *Think and Grow Rich* called "Three Feet from Gold." (If you don't know the story, google it.) Then they ask, "So what's the difference between tenacity and stupidity? Should I keep pushing through toward success, or am I just being stupid? And how can I tell the difference?"

This is a great question. Let me share an analogy for you to think about.

Imagine you are in a room that is attached to a second room beside it. You want to get into the second room. Both a tenacious and a stupid person might try to get into the other room by banging his head on the wall. That first attempt didn't work.

A tenacious person tries a different spot and bangs again—no result. A stupid person tries the original spot and bangs again—also no result. A tenacious person tries a new spot—bang! Again, no result. The stupid person bangs in the same spot again—still no result.

Another person enters the room and says, "I can show you another door to get into the other room." The tenacious person responds, "Really? Please show me."

The stupid person is approached by the same guide who knows where the door is and is invited to follow him to the door. The stupid person, however, says, "No, thanks, I'm good. I know what I'm doing." And they continue to bang their head again in exactly the same spot as before. No result.

What's the difference between a stupid person and a tenacious person? One is willing to change their approach and one is not. One is teachable and the other is not.

Most entrepreneurs fail or struggle because once again they feel like the answers for their business (and the profits too) must come exclusively from them. They aren't willing to accept help or learn from others who have gone through similar things before them. This is perhaps one of the biggest advantages my businesses have had. I was a committed learner even before I started my first business. I knew that I knew nothing and so I literally had nowhere to go but up.

As I teach entrepreneurs around the world, I see many who are teachable. These are generally the ones who succeed. They also aren't as concerned about who or where they learn from as long as the lessons will lead them and their businesses to higher levels. They are like sponges always looking for a better way to do things.

Those who have the opposite approach, however, of trying to discover all the answers themselves and doing everything in their business by themselves end up becoming frustrated and burning out, and they eventually either quit or settle for the life of continuous struggle.

Again, all of these things must show up in your personal life before they can show up in your business. If you think you are above getting help or are too smart to improve or do better, you've already lost.

There's a saying that I have found to be true in business and in life: If you want to expand what you have, you need to first expand who you are. You must set your own life in order before your business can follow.

You get to choose which category you will be in—stupid or tenacious. I can assure you one thing with certainty: you will never achieve a six-minute workday unless you become committed to constant improvement, including learning how to better utilize your time.

Exercise

Review your schedule and notice where you are spending too much time to get results that could be attained in more productive ways. Make a plan and a strategy for how you will do better in the upcoming week.

QUESTIONS: WHAT CAN BE DONE IN SIX MINUTES?

- How are you spending your time?
- How are you measuring how your time is spent?

- Can six minutes really make a difference? Why do you feel this way?
- What have you been able to accomplish in the past in a short period of time?
- How are you currently defining productivity?
- How can you use the funnel effect to make changes in your business and personal life?
- Where are you doing more when you should be seeking better?
- Are you tenacious or stupid?

Exercise

Consider the funnel effect. Where are you doing more with the intention to get more, but your efforts are resulting in less? Is there a way you can do better instead of doing more? Is there a way to create a situation where your productivity will be improved?

ACTION STEPS

1. Make a list of the activities you are currently doing to build your business. Identify both the long-term and short-term results that these activities are generating in your business. Knowing what gives you the most

impact and which tasks are most important will help you know where they fit in your schedule on a weekly basis. (Keep in mind that there are some activities that are necessary that don't always produce high levels of profit.)

2. Perhaps you want to start carrying around a stopwatch. You may not decide to put it on the table when you meet with others, but you may want to use it to start looking more carefully at all of the activities in your day. Where could you start being wiser with your time?

3. Yes, I want you to read *The 7 Habits of Highly Effective People* by Stephen Covey. In my opinion, it is one of the most important leadership, personal development, and business books ever written.

4. What habits in your life are a strength to your business, and which are a weakness? You don't have to get everything perfect, but you must know what tasks you will have to outsource and also which you may want to duplicate from your own experience. Early in my business career, I mostly hired people just like me. That means we magnified our strengths but also kept all of our weaknesses. We had a lot of holes in the company and this created a lot of problems. If you can determine your strengths and weaknesses regularly, you can heal them.

CHAPTER AHA MOMENTS

- Activities expand to fill the time you allow for them.
- Focused work is much more productive than work done over a long period of time with occasional focus.
- You teach people how to treat you.
- Be courteous, not casual, in your business relationships.
- Productivity is about doing better, not doing more.

Chapter 3

CREATING YOUR BUSINESS AND INCOME

To get to the goal of a six-minute workday, the most important step is to replace your financial freedom number. Naturally, I don't want you to stop there. I want you to raise to your financial abundance number.

Perhaps your goal as an entrepreneur is even greater. Perhaps you want to create a business that makes a bigger difference in your specific marketplace? Maybe you want to become a significant influencer in your market? Maybe you have a desire for fame and recognition in a new category? Maybe you want to pioneer a new way of doing things and a more effective way of thinking?

These are all fantastic goals. No matter how noble your goals are, you must make a profit if you are to stay in business. One of the business leaders I interviewed put it this way when it comes to business: "If you don't make a profit, you don't get the privilege to continue."

I have had several entrepreneurs over the years tell me that they aren't doing it for the money. Often, the people who say this don't last long. While the top entrepreneurs and business leaders I interviewed didn't always put profit as the primary goal in their organizations, it was definitely near the top.

In this chapter I will unfold a few formulas for how you can find balance in your pursuit of profit and still be empowered to make the differences you want to in your market and in the world.

THE 5 PILLARS OF WEALTH

To start, I want to take a look at where money is made. When you see how money is made in your organization, you can recognize more clearly how to best organize your business to support the most important aspects of your mission beyond profit. You've probably noticed that when people struggle with money, all they think about is money. However, when they have a plan in place around the money and they start to experience stability and success, they can shift their focus to other things.

Money and income flow through five primary areas. I call these the five pillars of wealth. They were taught to me while I was conducting my interviews with the top four hundred business leaders. They are essential for entrepreneurs, especially those just beginning, because understanding these pillars will help you know where to start and then how to stay focused as you build your empire.

These are the five pillars that form the foundations of wealth:

1. **Business:** This pillar refers to business enterprises and activities. This category could include starting a business from a concept and making it operational. It could also include buying an existing business or franchise. Business is often thought of as entrepreneurship; however, you can be an entrepreneur in any of these pillars. Business follows a unique structure that can be very different from the other pillars I will share. There are no ceilings or limitations to how profitable you may become. And it is often easier to sell a business to an interested third party than it is to sell the other pillars. More on this later. Do you want to build your six-minute workday as a business owner?

2. **Real Estate:** Real estate is the pillar where you are primarily focused on creating assets that can generate the income for you. Many people think that real estate

can be the easiest income source, but there are a lot of things to take into consideration (especially when you scale). Real estate is certainly the playground of entrepreneurs. Some think that it's not as risky as other wealth-building ventures because it is attached to a property, and thus a tangible asset, but that's not necessarily true. Real estate at scale has many moving parts. Yet when they are assembled correctly and managed properly, this can be one of the most rewarding and lucrative pillars. Do you want to build your six-minute workday in real estate?

3. **Investment:** I suppose real estate and business could both be considered forms of investment. In real estate you're investing in properties for profit and cashflow. In business you are investing in order to create more opportunities. The investment pillar refers to the movement of money. Your money, or the money of others, becomes your asset and employee. Through the movement and positioning of money, you are creating an income. Many people have created a six-minute workday in the field of money movement or investing. Do you want to build your six-minute workday in investing?

4. **Intellectual property:** Essentially, intellectual property is the selling of ideas. This has become extremely popular with the advent of technology. For example, there has been an explosion of people selling

courses and training online. But I want to expand your thinking on this pillar beyond the idea of creating an online course. Intellectual property can include the creation and licensing of your own ideas and creative works, and it can also include the selling and sharing of other people's ideas. You might remember the story of how at one point Michael Jackson owned the music catalog of The Beatles. He was paid millions in royalties on their songs, not The Beatles. There are scores of ideas that can be licensed or owned by people other than the original creators.

In addition, you can license your ideas or buy a license on someone else's ideas that will allow you to profit from the success of others. Lucasfilm, for instance, has never produced any toys connected to the blockbuster film *Star Wars*. Most likely you have seen the toys around anyway. That's because Lucasfilm has always sold the license to a third party. Why could you not acquire licenses or create the stories for others to pay you a license for?

A warning: If you are a content creator, you will have a hard time creating a six-minute workday because you'll always be creating. Just be aware of that. If you are a trader of intellectual property, you will be benefiting from the sharing of intellectual property that others have created and a six-minute workday will become more accessible. Do you want to build your six-minute workday through intellectual property?

5. **Networks:** More and more people are using their network to create their income stream. Perhaps the most visible example of this today are people who build and monetize big groups of followers or subscribers on a social media platform. This method is not the only way to build and monetize a network, however. For example, one of my students built a thriving network of subscribers around a printed political newsletter. He was able to turn this into a six-minute workday where the network actually carries most of the load. Another one of my students used the network principle to build a successful church group. Do you want to build your six-minute workday through networks?

I am confident that if you look closely at all of the successful entrepreneurial ventures that exist today, you will find at their roots one or more of these pillars.

Each of these pillars requires a level of skill to execute. But don't worry about that yet. I will show you how to gain those skills in the upcoming chapters. For now, consider which of these you would like to pursue.

Rodney sent me a thank-you note a few weeks ago. He thought he would be cut out for real estate. Everyone told him this was the best way to get rich, so that's what he decided he needed to do. But the truth is that he always had a hard time feeling comfortable asking his tenants for rent money or getting a damage deposit. When it came time to evict someone, he just didn't have the heart. While he was the owner of his properties on paper, he always felt like the tenants were the ones in control and he dreaded conversations with them. When he learned about the five pillars, he decided that real estate wasn't really for him and he began to look at and learn about investing. He was excited when he saw that he could make money with his own money and that the types of interactions investing requires were more aligned with how he wanted to conduct his relationships.

It is important to recognize that each of these pillars can become a six-minute workday. In my experience, each of them has a slightly different path to get there and some may take a little more effort and time in building the appropriate foundations to allow you to enjoy the six-minute workday. But I encourage you to look for the one that really speaks to you rather than searching for the one that will get you to the six-minute workday quicker.

Personally, I have diversified to include each of the five pillars in my life. But I also started with one. I encourage you to do the same. As I have helped my students around the world build in each of these pillars, I have found that some people have special gifts and talents that help them succeed more easily in some of the categories while they aren't as strong in others.

Look for what I call the low-hanging fruit. Warren Buffett once made a profound observation:

> "The interesting thing about business, it's not like the Olympics. In the Olympics, you know, if you do some dive off the—on a high board and have four or five twists—on the way down, and you go in the water a little bad, there's a degree of difficulty factor. So you'll get more points than some guy that just does a little head-first dive in perfectly.
>
> So degree of difficulty counts in the Olympics. It doesn't count in business. Now, you don't get any extra points for the fact that something's very hard to do. So you might as well just step over one-foot bars instead of trying to jump over seven-foot bars." (Taken from a CNBC interview, October 18, 2010)

Your goal should be to do the easy and simple thing to get started. Aim for the low-hanging fruit. Keep this in mind as you select the pillar that you're going to start with to build your empire.

Here are a few important things to think about as you go about building your pillar:

Ownership and Control Are Essential

To build your chosen pillar and establish a six-minute work-day that supports it, you will need ownership and control of the pillar. Ownership and control gives you the ability to make important decisions that will move you into the six-minute workday possibility. When there are multiple partners or a board of directors, they often try to create the enterprise in traditional ways. Most people only know the approach of trading time for money. Ownership will also give you the ability to sell the enterprise in the future if you wish to do so. We will return to the idea of ownership in greater detail in the next chapter.

Your Passion and Purpose Should Overlap with Others' Passions and Purposes

You've probably heard a million times some guru or business coach saying that you will be highly successful if you just follow your passion and purpose in business. The reality is that there are a lot of things people are passionate about that would never be a good company. In our live seminars I often use this example: If your passion and purpose was to coordinate your Beanie Baby collection, who would be interested in getting involved in that as a client? There may be a few, but you'd soon have no customers.

You cannot hope to be successful if you are exclusively focused on your passion and purpose. Quoting Warren Buffett once again, "What you love about you is your hobby. What others love about you is your business."

Rather than focus on your passion and purpose, you need to discover where your passion and purpose overlaps with that of others. The sweet spot in business and the area of most profit is where your passion and purpose overlaps the passion and purpose of those you want to serve. In this space is where you will not only be most profitable, but you will have the most ease in building the business. You will also have a sense of mission and validation, from which you'll draw great stamina and reward in serving this group. And you will attract those with whom the business resonates and they will help you grow the business.

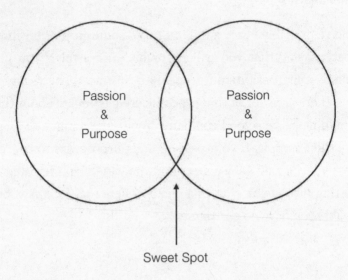

Passion & Purpose

Passion & Purpose

Sweet Spot

Olive is one of my students and she is an author and life coach. For years she was trying to find a way to get people excited about her perspectives on life and her unique approaches. She was trying very hard to convince people that she was on an enlightened path. It wasn't working very well. She was convinced her passion would convert them to her way of thinking. Things changed for her as soon as she discovered the idea of finding people who already had this same perspective, passion, and purpose. She was no longer in a constant state of trying to prove her worthiness to an unreceptive group. She was able to simply share her brilliance with a group that understood where she was coming from. Her online trainings began to fill up, and those in her tribe began sending her their friends who felt the same way.

You Need to Have More Than a Good Story

Recently, I saw an episode of *Shark Tank* during which an entrepreneur tried to tell one of the sharks that entrepreneurial success needs to be attached to a story. He tried to unravel this big argument about how people buy from those whom they like and understand. There may be a little bit of truth to that, but I doubt that it's the biggest motivator. I don't know about you, but I wouldn't necessarily buy from a company that gave a portion of their proceeds to a charity if I didn't like the product. For example, I support the mission of TOMS shoes, which donates a pair of shoes for every one purchased.

I wouldn't buy a pair of TOMS shoes unless I actually liked the shoes. And if they choose to donate, that's fine with me. But I won't buy a pair of shoes unless I intend to wear them. Be careful about putting too much weight in a story and expecting massive results. Your product or service needs to have an audience as well. There is a place for story, but it's not on the frontlines.

Identify Your Competition

I've met a lot of entrepreneurs who have told me that they have an idea so original that it doesn't have any competition. When I hear this, I become immediately worried. Either one of two possible things is happening here. One, they may truly have no competition, which tells me there may be very little interest in what they want to pursue. Perhaps there is no need or no interest from the public. That means that they are going to have a hard time creating an income. Most often when I hear the "no competition" line, it generally means the second possibility is happening: The entrepreneur has not done enough research into their market to know that they are not alone. They are usually surprised to see their idea already exists and sometimes that the competition is already doing a better job than they could; plus, they are both well positioned and funded.

When this happens, I don't encourage them to quit and I wouldn't tell you that either. Instead, I want you to consider two choices: collaborate with your competitors or master every part of your business. Take a careful look at the word *compete*. It suggests the idea of going head-to-head with someone. Strength against strength. Look for a way to best them through price dropping, quality, speed, diversity, and so on. Competing in this way often leaves both companies involved fighting and struggling for market share. I would suggest the answer is in adding one letter to the word *compete*. Turn the word *compete* into *complete*, and you now have a potential collaborator instead of a competitor.

Ask what you can do to add to the offer or improve the offer that already exists. What do the customers need before, during, or even after they have done business with your competitors?

I have personally experienced very effective results as I have collaborated with my competitors. They have genuinely become strong team players in my business as they have brought customers, increased word of mouth, marketed for me, and even bought me out handsomely.

Collaboration is the new economy.

The second consideration with a competitor is a saying we share at my training Entrepreneur of Influence. The saying is simple: mastery equals monopoly. What do I mean by that? As you become better at what you do, the completion of your competition thins out. The better you are, the fewer people there are that will compete with you at the highest level.

As you find ways to have better products, better systems, better marketing, better everything, people will choose to do business with you rather than your competitors. Your high quality builds a monopoly for you. Always strive for excellence. (Definitely more on this subject later.)

Stay Specific and Focused

Once you have fully considered the five wealth pillars, I encourage you to think about getting more focused. You can't be all things to everyone. I'll never forget the entrepreneur I met a few years ago at a networking event. He gave me his business card. One side listed four very different ventures, complete with logos. On the other side, squished around his contact information, were the names of three more companies. I remember being extremely confused as he gave me his card. These ventures were all so different. As I politely put the card into my pocket, I heard the expression "jack of all trades, master of none" pass through my brain. This guy certainly qualified. I already knew I wouldn't do any business with him.

I have since thought about this. Whenever I go to a networking event or look for someone to do business with, I am always on the hunt for the best support my money can buy. Pardon my honesty, but I am never looking for a jack of all trades or a person just kind of flirting with something to help me. I would never put my business in the hands of someone without focus.

Perhaps you've heard the idea that a millionaire has a minimum of seven income streams. Maybe this has got you thinking that you should build more than one wealth pillar up front to make things happen for you more quickly. If you do a little research, though, you'll see that millionaires' income streams are built one at a time with care. Or, these multiple income streams are all connected to a single pillar. Take your time and build things right in the beginning; there will be plenty of time to create more income streams once the first becomes stronger.

Think of it like the roots of a tree. You want the roots to grow solid and deep. Have you ever noticed that a baby tree requires more attention, even additional support? But as the roots grow deep and the trunk becomes solid, the tree can stand on its own. I never see a gardener out in the forest watering the mighty oak trees. They generally can take care of themselves once they reach a certain grandeur. Your business will be the same—aim for that.

I was chatting the other day with my friend Chris Browne. You may know him as the cofounder of Ted Baker. He shared that when they launched Ted Baker, they had put everything into it. As we talked about the idea of putting everything into your business, we both laughed as we realized we have never heard of a successful entrepreneur who said, "My company is a massive success and I only had to give it my attention occasionally."

For those of you who just read that and thought, *Whoa! I thought this book was about creating a six-minute workday*, I want to remind you that the early days will require more than six minutes. You will have to be ALL IN! And even when your six-minute workday is up and running, there will be lots of help making sure your venture gets all the attention it needs.

QUESTIONS: CREATING YOUR BUSINESS AND INCOME

- Which of the five pillars of wealth are you most interested to build in?
- Where have you observed pillars among other entrepreneurs?
- Do you own and control your pillar?
- How does your passion and purpose overlap the passion and purpose of those you want to serve?
- Who are your competitors in this marketplace? How can you collaborate with them? How can you become more valuable than them?
- Where is your focus?

ACTION STEPS

1. Consider the five pillars of wealth and select one of these that you will focus your efforts on. You may notice a few of these may overlap; however, I

encourage you to select the dominant description of what you are endeavoring to do. Remember there will come a time when you will have to describe your activities to others to get help. Once you have identified your specific pillar, I invite you to take some time and consider why you have chosen this specific area.

2. After you have chosen your pillar, remember the invitation to learn everything you can about it. What you learn will always affect what you are able to earn. And if you don't know it, you can't work with it. In your beginning stages I want to encourage you to spend a significant amount of time becoming an expert in this category. Now is not the time to expect the six-minute workday. You are still laying the foundations.

3. To develop greater mastery in your business, involve your customers in developing the best business you can create. Always carefully observe where your competitors are heading in the marketplace and consider why they would be choosing this direction. What is it they are trying to become better or more proficient at? Remember, however, that it is the customers' opinions that always matter most. There is no purpose in creating an innovation without customer appreciation.

CHAPTER AHA MOMENTS

- All successful companies can be reduced to a wealth pillar principle.
- Passion and purpose is secondary to validation and profitability.
- Competitors can be your greatest collaborators.
- Collaboration is the new economy.
- Mastery equals monopoly.
- Don't get lost in the story of your business.
- Focus on the business.
- Focus on one business.

Chapter 4

TRANSACTIONS–THE FOUNDATION OF BUSINESS

A few years into my interviews with top achievers and entrepreneurs, I was ready to start my own business. At the time I was regularly meeting with multimillionaires and billionaires and hearing the incredibly inspiring stories of how they had built their empires. Each time I met with someone new, my excitement and enthusiasm grew. I knew that entrepreneurship would be my path in life and I couldn't wait to get started.

One afternoon while I was meeting with one of these leaders, I mentioned that I was now ready to start building a venture of my own. To my surprise, not only was he encouraging but he also asked for the opportunity to be one of the first to look at the business as a potential investor. This was one of the most exciting moments of my life up until that point.

As we talked more about my new venture, I asked him what he might need to see to consider becoming an investor. His answer was simply that he would like to see a business plan. Although I had never built one before, I was pretty confident I could assemble one. We set an appointment for a week away and I left his offices that day excited to begin working on my business plan.

I looked online and in libraries to figure out what elements my business plan should include to increase my chances of success. Within a short time, I started graphing out timelines, marketing plans, charts about demographics, and everything else that I could think of that would indicate that I knew what I was doing. As I got to the twenty-four-hour copy center near my home, I saw all the options for printing, binding, and lamination. I was committed to making this the best and most complete business plan my investor friend had ever seen.

As the business plan grew in thickness, my confidence also rose. I decided foolishly then that the thicker this plan was, the smarter it would make me. I started to include everything that made even the slightest bit of sense.

By the time I was finished, it was close to three o'clock in the morning and I had a bound document over three inches thick. I was excited.

I entered my potential investor's office and his secretary asked me to take a seat. He soon came into the lobby to greet me, and when I displayed the three-inch-thick business plan, he gave the "Wow! You've been busy" reaction that I was hoping for.

Once in his office, I set the business plan on his desk for him to get another good look. I was really hoping he would remark that I was destined to be a success and I was certainly a business prodigy. Instead, after again congratulating me on my hard work, he asked a question without even opening the business plan: "So, what are the main transactions?"

I smiled. I hadn't heard that one before.

I started to talk a bit about my major demographic, hoping that somewhere in my ramblings he would find the answer. After about a minute, he smiled and asked the question again.

"What is your key transaction?"

I worried that he sensed I was lost. (Which, of course, I was.) I began this time to talk about my clever marketing strategy. How I could out-position others in the marketplace through the use of some unique and creative ads.

He smiled again and asked the question once more: "What are the transactions?"

Without missing a beat, I tried to cover up my lack of knowledge again by deflecting his question with details from another part of my business plan: the distribution model.

This time I knew I was caught. He simply said, "You don't know what I mean by transaction, do you?"

My silence betrayed me. He then took out a piece of paper and drew a diagram for me. On one side was the word *company*. He said this represented me. On the other side, he wrote the word *customer*.

He then drew one arching arrow at the top, from the company to the customer. And then another arching arrow underneath, from the customer to the company. Beside this he drew a dollar sign.

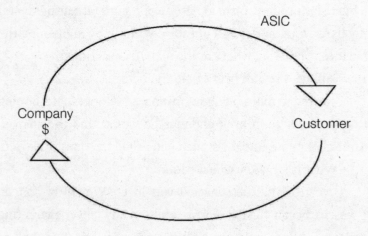

He explained that a transaction is what you will give the customers in exchange for their money. He said that this simple diagram is the beginning of all business success. I could write pages and pages covering demographics, marketing, and distribution, but none of this mattered if I didn't understand the transaction. The transaction is the foundation of the entire business.

- I wouldn't find the right demographic until I understood the transaction.
- Marketing was a waste of time until I understood the call to action I would need to use to engage customers in the transaction.
- And things like distribution and manufacturing really didn't matter until I knew what the core transaction was.

As we spoke about transactions, and I learned more about this incredible concept, my mentor and I talked about the importance of identifying all the steps that are required for a transaction to occur. I will talk more about this later on in the book and you can also find a version of this diagram at www .SixMinuteWorkday.com that will help you start to build out your business in a way that will help you turn it into a prosperous six-minute workday venture. Be sure to get that chart.

Since that time, I have come to realize that the transaction diagram fits with all of the five wealth pillars we spoke about in the previous chapter.

In addition, it has become clear that if you consider what the customer will receive from the company, there can only be three options for what you can sell: an asset, a service, or information.

An **asset** is a tangible product that you deliver into the hands of your customer. In a business, the product could be any kind of widget or creation. In real estate, the asset is the property itself. In investing, stocks or share certificates are types of assets. In intellectual property, it could be a product or recording. In networks, it could be a physical list of leads. You get the idea.

A **service** is any kind of activity that is done to support the customer. Your business could be housecleaning. A real estate service might entail the rental of a storage unit. Providing financing would be an investment service. Intellectual property services could involve problem solving or consulting. Making introductions might be your networking service. Easy, right?

Information is pretty self-explanatory. You are selling knowledge. Pretty much everything in this category could be considered intellectual property although you could sell knowledge in each of the five pillars.

Those three things—assets, service, and information—are really the only three things you can sell. When you start to put together the pillars, the transaction, and what you will sell, you will start to see your entrepreneurial venture taking shape.

ESTABLISHING YOUR TRANSACTION

Let's go back for a minute to the transaction diagram. As I mentioned above, there are certain things that will have to happen for your customer to receive the asset, service, or information you are selling and for you to receive the money they pay for it.

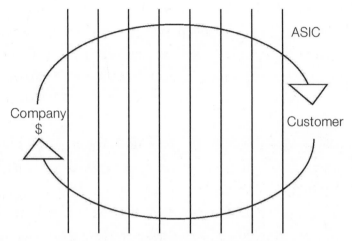

Elements that are required to create the transaction.

Before we get into those things, let's talk a little about the purchase itself.

Fair Exchange of Value

Perhaps you've heard of a principle called fair exchange of value when it comes to getting your customers to participate in your transaction. There are a lot of business coaches and so-called entrepreneur trainers throwing around this term today. Most of them don't get it. Customers are not really that interested in a fair exchange of value (at least not in the way these folks are describing it). Fair exchange of value is generally thought of as simply creating a deal that works well for both the company and the customer. Creating something that's basically, well, fair.

But let's take a closer look at it and you'll see why it doesn't work. Let's say you have an asset that is worth one dollar. You created it for a dollar, it has one dollar's worth of your time in it, and so it seems fair to say that it is worth a single dollar.

Now put yourself in the shoes of a customer. If I came to you and presented you a dollar bill and asked you to pay a dollar for it, would you?

Most likely not. Why not? Well, because it doesn't really make sense to trade a dollar for a dollar. No one wins, no one gains. It's basically a waste of time and effort for all involved. I believe this is why so many businesses struggle to have great success and booming sales. Most of them are asking their customers to simply trade a dollar for a dollar.

Now put yourself back into the shoes of the customer. When you have purchased something, why did you buy it?

It's likely because whatever you bought seemed to provide you with more value than its cost. If something cost a dollar, you paid that dollar because you felt that the value you were receiving back was worth at least two dollars, maybe three, or maybe more. The value you gained gave you the ability to feel good, look better, earn more money, have more power, made you feel sexier, and otherwise gave you more satisfaction than the dollar that it cost you. Perhaps you can start to see where I am going with this. People never spend a dollar unless they feel they are getting more value in return.

So far, this idea sounds great. That is until you get to the idea that this exchange is very much slanted in the direction of the customer. No business can afford to give customers three dollars' worth of value for only a dollar and expect to stay in business long term, right?

Perhaps that's where we need to stop and talk about the other side of the equation.

For your business to be happy accepting a dollar from your customer, you need to find a way to create an offering that costs you less than a dollar, but still leaves the customer feeling like they receive a great deal.

When you can find this balance, then you have a true fair exchange of value.

Lots of companies have been able to find out how to do this. The challenge is that there are so many fair offers in the marketplace. Fair offers don't really create a "wow" experience. Nobody ever takes the time to tell their friends about a fair exchange or an expected offer. They will, however, take the time to tell people when they get an incredible deal.

Your goal, then, is not to create fair exchanges, but to deliver intense "wow" experiences that build your client base. When you are building out the transactions you want to create in your business, you need to understand that the more irresistible and sustainable you make your offers the more transactions you will have, and ultimately your transactions determine your profit.

For example, would you rather have ten thousand transactions from which you made a dollar, or complete one hundred transactions from which you made $1,000? If you did the math correctly, you would take the fewer transactions with the higher sale value: $10,000 versus $100,000, right?

What would happen if you were able to scale those original one hundred transactions to ten thousand transactions, but the price point of $1,000 stays the same? Now you are looking at $10,000,000.

Scale is more about the number and size of the transactions you will do than the number of locations or countries you serve. Scaling is all about increasing the number of successful transactions.

Wilson had spent quite a bit of money trying to build more locations and find people to fill them. The transactions per employee was his measure of success. His impression was that the fastest way to grow profits was simply to get more hands helping. When he realized that the principle of scale had to do specifically with the number of transactions instead of the people creating them, a light bulb went off. He began to devote some time to discovering how his transactions were really being generated and where his clients were coming from. He also took a careful look at what other needs his customers had

and created some additional products to serve them. Within a
short period of time, his profits tripled.

The Three Parts of a Transaction

If the business scale is determined by the number of transactions, it is essential that we really understand as much as
we can about how these transactions are going to be built,
because the better we understand our transaction at this level,
the easier it will be to build our six-minute workday.

Understanding the transaction will assist us in getting
help to build our business, serve our customers, determine
how and where to expand, and even when to pivot.

You'll remember I mentioned that for the customer to give
you money and for you to deliver an asset, service, or information to them, there will be certain steps that need to happen.

These steps can be divided into three primary areas. These
three areas do not include several business essentials that are
often hidden from the customer's view, such as business operations, staff training, management, bookkeeping, accounting,
and other similar details. Though not discussed specifically,
you'll see that many of these things fit into these primary areas.

The three major areas are what I call TELL, SELL, and
SERVICE.

Tell: The things you will have to do to tell your customer
about the offering can include marketing, branding,

public relations, and so forth. This area really contains everything that is associated with how your customers hear about you and the messaging that is contained in that communication.

Sell: These aspects of your transaction are focused not only on the actual sale but the transfer of asset, service, and information into the customer's hands and the transfer of money into your hands. This can include the actual sales process, delivery, and even collections. When someone appreciates your offer and wants to do business with your company, this is the step that allows them to continue the relationship with you. One of my mentors once said to me that "In business nothing really happens until a sale is made." I would agree with that statement.

It's also worth pointing out that the easier you can make the selling process, the more sales you will have. You should be on a constant mission to improve this area of your transactions.

Service: Service is what happens after the sale. It can include elements of delivery, but it is actually more focused on what occurs after delivery. What support is available for your customers? How can they continue to feel good about their experience with you? Does your service process encourage people to buy again or refer you to their friends?

These steps are going to become the foundation of your systems and the kinds of support you will have to acquire to be able to shift from a full workday and embrace the six-minute workday structure. Take time to fully understand these elements of the transaction.

It's also important that you understand that the way these elements unfold in the transaction today may not be the same as how they will in the future. Technology and the marketplace are constantly changing. The reason for a customer to purchase today may shift entirely or new innovations may require a massive pivot. In 2020, as the COVID-19 pandemic swept the world, there were massive shifts in how people did business. While many people were ready and could pivot quickly, there were many who could not. And as a result their businesses closed their doors. I believe one of the biggest reasons these businesses failed is because they did not understand the transactions their companies were engaged in and so they didn't know what steps to take to shift and maintain their transactions through telling, selling, and offering service.

Challenges in the marketplace always reveal who is lucky and who really knows what they are doing. Don't leave your success to chance.

THE SEQUENCE OF SUCCESS

Up until now, we have been really focused on the concept of transaction and rightly so. Most people make the mistake of thinking that the transaction is all about profits and making money. The reality is that the company and the customer must have a relationship before money can enter the picture. Think about the diagram showing the exchange between company and customer—even that sequence has many lessons.

Most businesses that fail look at the transaction and build things by first focusing on the money. Recently I was speaking with a new business coach who wanted my help to grow his business. I started by asking him to tell me about his programs. He began by simply saying that he "had one for $97 for beginners, then they moved up to a $497 course, and then there was a $5,000 coaching program."

I instantly realized the reason for his business struggles. His perspective was to start by sharing what something cost and he based his prices on what he had seen his competitors charging. The reality is that your customers and mine do not buy something just because we share a price. I asked him to tell me about his programs, and he described what he would do at each level.

At the $97 level you will get a book and video series that I wrote. At the $497 level you will get access to a four-module video course, and at the $5,000 level you will get a weekly, one-hour phone call with me for a month.

He seemed satisfied, but I was not. No one buys things based on how they are built or how many hours they get. It's not enough. In this messaging there's no real connection to how the product or service will help customers. People don't buy processes, they buy results.

Think about it. When you pull into the drive-through, did you come to get a cheeseburger or did you pull in so you could wait behind another car, talk into the squawky box to place your order, drive up to the window, and so forth? You got in the line for the cheeseburger. You only wanted the results and you are not interested in the other aspects of the experience.

As I talked to this business coach about this, he started to get the message. I asked him to describe what his customers would actually get and what they would be able to do at each of the levels he offered. What would their results be?

To answer this question, he needed to follow the sequence of success: people, then product, then profits.

To identify your sequence of success, start by thinking about how your transactions help people. Go back to that idea of exchange of value and creating irresistible offers. How are you creating offers that speak to the desires of your customers and helping them achieve their desired results? After you see clearly what they really want to achieve or feel or be, then you would do well to share products that help them achieve those goals.

Through the products, they can see how their goal will be accomplished. Showing them the products is like showing them the road and the car that will take them to their dream destination.

If you share focus on the result these people will experience and help them see that your products will take them there, you will get your profits.

When you are searching for a business coach or someone to support your business, you should be careful. While there are lots of well-meaning people out there who call themselves consultants, most have never built or been a part of big business before. Even though they may have good intentions to help you, they may not have the ability. The three most important things that most people never consider when hiring someone to support their business are:

1. Do they have experience with your specific pillar (business, real estate, investment, intellectual property, or networks)?
2. Have they achieved a high level of success and are they still doing it? (Old information won't really help you in a marketplace that is moving at an ever-increasing pace.)
3. Do they have the network that can support your growth? Remember that all strong business is built through associations and network. This business is your venture. Don't put yourself in a bad position by getting bad support.

QUESTIONS: TRANSACTIONS— THE FOUNDATION OF BUSINESS

- What are your core transactions?
- How are you keeping the transaction at the center of your business focus?
- What does fair exchange of value look like to your customer?
- What does a fair exchange of value look like to you?
- How can you create a fair exchange of value?
- How do you scale a company?
- How are you currently telling people about you?
- How are your customers able to continue the relationship?
- How is your sales process structured?
- How are you providing service for your customers?
- What does service mean to you?
- How do your products support the results customers are looking for?
- How have you been losing sales by putting profits first?

ACTION STEPS

1. As you get ready to start building your six-minute workday, make a list of all the things that need to happen in the categories of Tell, Sell, and Service to

facilitate your transactions. The more you know about what needs to be done to facilitate the transaction, the better. It is also important to recognize which specific activities are most important, and you can even start labeling them in terms of priority. I invite you to start making this list now so that you can be ready as we get to the next phase of building your six-minute workday!

2. It's a good idea to start to really understand your marketplace. Make a list of the competitors who are currently selling in this category and take a look at where they are actually making their money.

3. Consider carefully: What is the transaction you are trying to create? Dumb it down into the smallest and most precise action you can. This transaction is going to be your guiding goal in all you do.

4. Take some time to understand from your customer what they truly find valuable about your transaction offerings. How can you make your offering more valuable to them without spending more time or money to create that offering?

CHAPTER AHA MOMENTS

- The size of your business plan means nothing.
- If you can't explain your mission in a sound bite, you don't have one.
- The transaction you are trying to create must guide every other aspect of the business.
- Customers look for a good deal, not a fair deal.
- Irresistible offers aren't necessarily more expensive—they just target the value better.
- The number of transactions will always directly affect the profitability of your company.
- Scale is about the number of transactions.
- People buy results, not processes.
- Your sequence of success is: people, then products, then profits.

Part 2

CREATING YOUR
6-MINUTE WORK DAY

IIIII

Chapter 5

THE 3 PHASES OF CREATING YOUR 6-MINUTE WORK DAY

Now that we have the foundational principles covered, it's important that we start talking about how to shift from a full workday to the six-minute workday. When I am sharing this particular step with students at my seminars, it doesn't take long for someone to realize that the idea of condensing a full workday into just six minutes is often called a passive income lifestyle.

This is true. When you can shift to a six-minute workday, you are actually talking about creating a passive income lifestyle. Perhaps the reason I don't just come out and say *passive income* is because most people don't really understand what that term means and they equate it with all kinds of false ideas and notions.

For example, most people think passive income means sketchy and get-rich-quick business models. The reality is that all businesses are built on the principles of passive income and, when they are done right, you get paid for transactions that you did not create or supervise. More on that in a minute.

I've also heard people talking about passive income as something new that happens only online—that you need to have a specific set of technical skills to make it work and even then it's a rare thing when it does. The reality is that passive income has always been a part of doing business. While it can be made with the help of technology—like the internet—it doesn't always require it. A great couple of examples I like to point out include collecting rent on a property (in this case, it's the asset doing the work and you aren't really doing much) or lending out money and collecting interest (here, the money is doing the work and there's not really much that you have to do to get paid).

Another false idea about passive income is that if it's too good to be true, then it probably is. But what those who say this don't realize is that it does involve a fair amount of work. There is quite a bit of effort required to get things set up to generate the passive income; it doesn't happen automatically.

A more accurate description of this type of income would be to call it *income passive*. This term acknowledges that the income and systems are set up first, which results in a passive lifestyle. The most accurate description, however, and the one I choose to use, is *leveraged income.*

We all understand the idea of leverage. Perhaps we've even used it as a kid. If we wanted to move a big rock out of its place, we found a stick and used it as a lever. That lever, applied in the correct way, gave the needed strength to move the rock.

It was the philosopher Archimedes who is credited with saying, "Give me a place to stand, and a lever long enough, and I will move the world."

All wealth and freedom are created through the use of leverage. But this leverage doesn't appear instantly. It's important to understand the effort involved in building leverage so as to manage your expectations as you begin to shift toward a six-minute workday.

We've already talked about a few things that you will have to do, and some of these things will take significant time and effort. They are not impossible and they are not beyond what someone could do as a side hustle. I have had thousands of students from nearly every country who have been able to benefit from and expand their businesses by building these foundations and then applying leverage.

WHAT IS LEVERAGE?

Leverage is the use of systems, and putting systems in place is how you are going to establish a six-minute workday. You are going to use systems to liberate you from trading time for money. There are really only two systems you can use: delegation and automation.

Delegation is using the skills, talents, knowledge, labor, time, and efforts of other people to create your transactions. You'll remember in the last chapter we talked about all the steps that need to be accomplished for the transaction to occur. Well, the first set of systems that you will start using to shift the activity in those transactions from your efforts to others is delegation. I know it sounds simple, but stick with me and I'll show you the process by which it is going to be done.

The second way systems are built is through automation, technology, and existing systems. I am not just referring to the internet but to all forms of technology and automation. This can also include using systems that other people have created. For example, if the wealth pillar that you've selected is real estate, you may choose to use the system that has been built by a property management company. That existing system could take care of everything from maintenance to collecting the rent to finding tenants. I am going to talk a lot more about automation, technology, and existing systems in future chapters because these are key to achieving a six-minute workday.

There is a procedure and method to effectively combining these systems to create your six-minute workday, and much of the remainder of this book will be focused on that. I want to stress that what I have been sharing so far is not theory or some crazy pie-in-the-sky dream. This is what I do, what many of my students have done, and what you will be able to do too. But you need to have correct expectations for the next steps so that when things don't come easily—and they won't—you won't become discouraged and quit, saying that what I have shared doesn't work.

In the following chapters we are going to talk about the three steps of using effective leverage to give you the six-minute workday in a way that works and in a way that you can maintain. I want to outline those expectations here so that you can understand what is possibly ahead for you. My intention in writing this book is to give you what you need to create a six-minute workday, so please do something with the formula I am about to unfold.

Pay careful attention, as surprises and incorrect expectations are often what cause entrepreneurs to fail. If you know what's coming, you can get committed in advance and keep going. When things you expect appear, you will know you are on track and they will confirm you are on your way rather than cause you to doubt, fear, fail, and quit.

PHASE 1—CREATION

Creation is the first part of creating the six-minute workday. I promise you that this part will not be accomplished in six minutes per day. It will definitely require much more time, effort, planning, correction, and consistency. Think of it like planting the seeds. You will have to select the seeds, select the appropriate ground, monitor these fragile seeds as they are planted, and make adjustments to ensure their survival. There may be long hours and early mornings. Here you are going to identify what systems need to be created and how you will get the help of others, technology, and existing systems to ensure delegation and automation down the line.

At this stage and along the way, you may find some of the systems you have brought in are not the best for the job. New systems may have to be tried while some may have to be modified or even discarded. Some systems will be brilliant as you launch but will soon have to be replaced.

You will have to be very involved at this phase of the business. Sometimes I see entrepreneurs who are too quick to pass the reins off to someone else and then the business quickly fails. You have to shift from this stage to the next stage very carefully. It's like the game you may have played as a kid where you are running a race trying to balance an egg in a spoon that you hold in your mouth. As you transfer the egg to the next stage, you will need to be very careful and focused or you may just have to start again at zero.

This stage is often the most expensive as well. Yet you don't want to skimp on costs because it must be done right. You need to be correctly set up legally. You need to establish structures for your company—the agreements for bringing people on board and for record keeping. You will also need your financial professionals to help you get organized so that you are not paying too much in taxes and so that you can do proper projections and calculations. You also need to have proper help in creating branding and a company image. You only get one chance to make a first impression.

It is for these reasons and others that this stage can often be the most expensive. And the most challenging part is that many of these expenses must be paid before you start making any money. We'll talk about some strategies you can use to improve your chances of success in the chapters ahead.

Expectations for the Creation Phase

- *This stage generally requires three to twelve hours of work per day.*
- *On average this stage takes three months to three years to go through.*
- *Generally speaking, this stage is financially tough and profits, if there are any, are small.*

Nate was a serial entrepreneur who kept continually creating new ventures. Everything he touched seemed to prosper . . . at least for a while. When we met, he expressed this as a reoccurring challenge. As we looked closer at the situation, we discovered that he was suffering with something that so many other entrepreneurs struggle with—the creation cycle. The creation cycle occurs when an entrepreneur doesn't know how to shift from the creation phase of the company to the next stage, which we will discuss shortly. When an entrepreneur doesn't know how get to the next phase, they are destined to repeat the phase they have mastered again and again. Keep reading and you'll see how we were able to help Nate finally create a venture that progressed into a sustainable and growing business.

I had a conversation with Joe Foster a while back. Joe cofounded Reebok. It was interesting to talk to him about the creation stage of Reebok. There were a lot of challenges and a lot of things that worked out serendipitously. One of my favorite stories was how they came up with the name. (I won't give away the punch line and the dramatic reveal. But you definitely want to check it out.)

The creation phase is such a fun stage with so many happy accidents and lucky breaks. As I interviewed the top business leaders, one of the things that I found in common among all of them was that they all delighted in the opportunity to share stories from this part of their business journey.

Enjoy this stage and look for the fun moments. Brian Smith, founder of UGG boots, once shared with me that he felt the biggest challenge that most entrepreneurs face is that they try to speed things along and get to success without enjoying where they are at the present moment—staying in the now. Brian's words were, "Be content to be a tadpole. Don't rush to become a frog."

PHASE 2–MAINTAIN

Now that you have graduated from the creation phase, you will find that you actually do start seeing some time freedom appear. At this stage the systems that you implemented in the creation phase are starting to find their way. The initial fire you started is beginning to take hold and turn into a fire of its own.

Because you have been so involved in the creation phase, it feels bizarre to begin to step back. One of my friends made this joke. He said that a successful business in the future will be made up of three elements: a computer, a person, and a dog. The man will set up the computer and then the dog will be required to keep him from touching it again. Too often people at this stage keep fiddling with the company and the systems they've set up as if they are still in the creation phase. As a result, they screw everything up.

You have hired smart people and built good systems in the creation phase, and you need to get out of the way and allow them to begin to do their work.

You may have heard this insightful saying: If you are a cog in the wheel, you are a clog in the wheel. Let the wheel you have built do its thing. In chapter 7, I will share some other challenges that many entrepreneurs experience as they are at this stage of their workday creation.

In this phase you will also start exploring partnerships, joint ventures, collaborations, hiring, and other ways to get people supporting and helping you. If this is not done with

clarity about the kind of support you need, you can find yourself in a lot of trouble. The moment you start getting other
people involved, things start getting complicated.

Nearly every one of the top business leaders I interviewed
expressed that the greatest moments and also the most challenging moments had to do with bringing people into their
companies. It was in those moments that they grew the most.
But at the same time, most of their troubles were attached to
bringing people into the company. In the pages to come, we
will talk about some of the challenges that may come your
way, how to prepare for them, and even how to prevent them
before they arise.

I often hear from entrepreneurs that they find this stage
gets tedious for them. I am not sure that I agree. I think that
those who find this stage boring aren't quite doing it right.
I have personally found this stage exciting as my company
shifted from fragile to flowing. Be sure to enjoy your time in
this stage.

Expectations for the Maintain Phase

- *This stage generally requires thirty minutes to three
  hours of work per day.*
- *On average, this stage can take six to nine months to go
  through.*
- *Generally speaking, modest profits begin to appear
  during this phase, but often they do not appear
  consistently. There will be good weeks and bad weeks.*

PHASE 3—EXPANSION AND CONTINUITY

This is the phase that I am at in most of my businesses. This is where you begin to experience a true six-minute workday (or some days no work at all). At this stage your role shifts to one of being the true entrepreneur. You are the conductor of the orchestra. Much of what is happening in your company is now automatic. You are in a flow. Some of my activities here are to look for new opportunities, ways to expand what I am already doing, hire new help, or look for additional systems. Certainly, at this point, I am in a state of measurement and looking for ways to improve, but I also have lots of help to do it.

Expansion is one of the most rewarding aspects of being an entrepreneur. I always love the moment when I encounter someone who has had a good experience with one of my brands. I also really love sharing that success with all who helped make it happen, including the customers. After all, isn't this a big reason why we do what we do?

One of the success interviews I conducted was with Frank Maguire, the former VP of marketing at American Airlines, KFC, and ABC. He was like a grandpa to me. We spent a lot of time together. What he's most known for is being one of the four founders of FedEx.

Before he passed away, I used to love spending hours listening to his stories about the rise of FedEx. He shared wisdom for growth and expansion and never giving up. Every time he would share one of the stories around the challenges FedEx faced in its early days, he would conclude with an exciting victory story that made it all seem worthwhile.

I suppose there is a powerful lesson in that. While you may have tough moments in building your business, the tough moments will eventually have a powerful victory story attached if you keep pushing through. No success is an accident. And even the most well-known international brands have had their share of challenges in growth.

It was interesting to see, as I spoke with Frank, that even FedEx went through these three phases. The creation phase was expensive and everyone was working like crazy to get the business running. In the first few years of creation, FedEx went through a ton of the investors' money and things didn't look promising.

But with perseverance they pushed through and were able to reach stability. They moved into a state of maintenance once everyone knew they were here to stay and their brand was established. Customers began to come to them, and return, en masse.

Eventually they were in a position where they had such strength that they could focus on expansion. Interestingly enough, Frank told me how at this stage he also had more time, got more help, had bigger budgets, and freedom began to appear.

It will be the same for you.

Expectations for the Expansion Phase
- *This stage generally requires a few minutes to an hour of work per day.*
- *On average, this stage can last for as long as you take care of it.*
- *Generally speaking, profits begin to grow exponentially here. Now that you know what you are doing and you monitor it correctly, there are few limits. This is literally where multimillionaire status can occur. There will be mostly good weeks and few surprises.*

(HOPEFULLY NOT) PHASE 4—REPAIR

It's important to point out that in Phase 4, I am still not stepping completely away from my business. I have met many entrepreneurs who get through Phases 1 and 2 and then they assume they can go on holidays. Sometimes those holidays can last for months or even years. But following neglect of their business like this, they will return from those holidays to find a dreaded Phase 4 that I believe can be avoided: Repair.

How do I know it exists? Because I've had to do it. In my city we have a really big rodeo that comes through once a year. It's called the Calgary Stampede. For about a week in July, nobody does any work. They are either at the fairgrounds or having some kind of office party. It really is the kickoff to summer. A few years ago, I thought my businesses were doing so well without me that I started my celebrations early in June. And while most people went back to work in mid-July, I kept playing until about October. (Yikes!)

Needless to say, I didn't really monitor my systems or the people helping me. As long as money was hitting my bank account somewhat regularly, I wasn't really that concerned. Sure, I took a look from time to time, and responded to the occasional question by email or phone, but mostly I just kind of let everything coast.

When I came back to my business that October, I was surprised to see that many people who were part of what I was doing had left (and some of them took money with them). One of them had started a side hustle with my customers. One of my systems was not functioning at all but I was still being billed for it. All in all, it was a terrible disaster.

Expectations for the Repair Phase

- *This generally is the hardest stage if you have to face it.*
- *Sometimes you can't repair a business or income stream. Sometimes the damage it creates can also be a very expensive—even life-destroying—event. During this time, there will mostly be a lot of bad weeks as you try to sort out everything that went wrong and salvage what still might be possible. There'll be lots of explanation owed to customers and you'll have to work to keep the good systems and people that you had. Count*

on making lots of phone calls and sending lots of emails
that often won't be well received.

I had no choice but to get to work with Phase 4: Repair. Repair is much more painful than creation. Sometimes repair means trying to fix more than broken systems. Sometimes it can mean trying to fix relationships and reputation. Having been there, I don't recommend it. It would have been so much easier for me to simply take the six minutes each day and do it correctly. I hope you learn from my lesson.

There's a reason why doctors keep checking the vital signs of their patients; it keeps them alive. And if you watch carefully, the monitors for the vital signs are always running. Even if they think the patient is doing okay. We will talk in more detail about how to monitor the vital signs of your business.

If you make a few mistakes along the way, it's all right. Even if you fumble the ball a little and have to make some repairs, that, too, is okay. No one has a perfect, polished, and pristine ride to the top. Every successful entrepreneur I ever interviewed and every great entrepreneur I have worked with has experienced moments where they have had to jump in and make some repairs. You will have that as well.

The best advice I was ever given about this was when you see a problem or a problem coming, get it fixed as quickly as you can. And remember: you don't fix anything by blaming others. We will talk more about ownership and control as we move forward, but remember that the most important things you can own are not your victories but your failures.

QUESTIONS: THE 3 PHASES OF CREATING YOUR 6-MINUTE WORK DAY

- In what way is passive income an old principle?
- What is leverage?
- Why is leverage important?
- What is a system? How can it help you with the principle of leverage?
- How are you checking the vital signs of your company? What are the three phases of the six-minute workday? Which phase are you in right now?
- Why do so many entrepreneurs struggle to shift between phases?
- How does owning failure help you to achieve higher profits?

ACTION STEPS

1. Get a mentor to help you correctly lay the foundations in Phase 1: Creation. Don't skimp on establishing legal ownership and protection at this stage either. You

need to make sure that all of your bases are covered in creation before getting others involved in your venture.

2. Start keeping careful notes on systems—delegating techniques and automation, technology, and the systems of others—that you see working in the world around you. Don't be overly concerned if the system you are observing has nothing to do with your marketplace or the wealth pillar you have chosen. Systems can often be adapted from other pillars to work elsewhere.

3. Take a moment and pick some of the big companies that you admire. Take a look at their history from concept to where they are today. Identify the different phases of creation, maintenance, and expansion in their story. What kinds of struggles did they have? What helped them to succeed quicker and long term? How did they build more stability in their ventures? How can you do the same?

CHAPTER AHA MOMENTS

- Leveraged income is how you will gain your freedom.
- Properly manage your expectations and get committed.
- Achieving a six-minute workday requires three phases of business growth. Don't rush through them.

- Some of your best stories in the future will come from the creation phase.
- All companies go through the three phases.
- Attention and consistency will prevent you from going through the fourth phase: repair.
- Every business will encounter some challenges—fix them as quickly as you can.

Chapter 6

PHASE 1—CREATION: AN ACTIVE BEGINNING

When a farmer plants a seed, it is an act of faith. He doesn't know what the future will bring for that little seed. But he has hope. He has hope that it will grow into the crop that he intends and he has hope it will provide the rewards that he intends.

The same is true of the creation aspect of business. The activities and efforts that we put in at this stage are a manifestation of the hope we have that the results will be what we intend.

I have worked with countless entrepreneurs around the world, and there have been those who are successful and those who have struggled and failed. Most commonly, the reason for failure has been attached to the beginning of the process.

Considering that your beginnings are the foundation of your six-minute workday, it is important that you take the time to begin correctly. Most entrepreneurs I share this with nod their head and say they agree, but it often becomes very hard for them because the beginning part often requires them to slow down just a little bit to build a good foundation.

I am glad, however, that the foundation is a little more complex and time consuming. I have noticed another thing with entrepreneurs, myself included. Most of us are idea people. We are creators. I read a statistic once that claimed the average person has six ideas per year that could turn into a multimillion-dollar business. Most entrepreneurs I know experience that in a single morning.

This version of entrepreneurial ADD (attention deficit disorder) often keeps them from creating success. Because of these new sparks of ideas constantly hitting them, many entrepreneurs are never focused enough to get something built. Perhaps you've experienced this. I know I have.

Sometimes I have simply gotten bored with an idea. Other times I have lost interest as I began to realize how complex the idea really is. Other times I have been discouraged as I began to confront challenges. Whatever the reason, most entrepreneurs experience the same feelings.

To be successful, we must stay focused and understand the law of gestation, which basically states that things take time. You can't get a baby to be born faster by setting up the crib in advance. You can't expect to graduate on the first day of school. All these things take a little time.

One of the mentors I learned from expressed it this way: Imagine being hungry and going into a restaurant. You sit down and order a steak. As the waiter leaves, you look at your watch. A minute has passed. Still no steak. So, you get up and go to another restaurant and repeat the same process of ordering. Again, another minute passes and you go to another restaurant and do the whole thing again. You leave that restaurant after a minute and repeat this same thing again elsewhere. And you keep doing this at hundreds of restaurants. Eventually you die of hunger, still never having eaten your steak.

As he finished this analogy, he warned me that most entrepreneurs are like this. To some extent, I was like this. The remedy that worked for me was to carry around a black notebook and put my business ideas inside. At the end of the week, I would look back and determine what my best ideas were and what I was most interested in. This separation of the excitement and enthusiasm around the idea and the idea itself by adding in a little bit of time before fully considering it has helped me to find what I really wanted to do.

I know other entrepreneurs who get so excited that every time they have an idea they go and buy the domain name. Some of them have hundreds or even thousands of domain names. Take some time and think about things before you begin, always keeping in mind that whatever business you choose will be in your life for a long time. Don't just chase something because it's a fad or you think you can make a quick buck.

A few basic questions you need to answer in getting started include:

- What is your business's transaction? (Go back to chapter 4 if you need some reminders on this one.)
- Is there going to be more than one transaction? (I recommend yes!)
- Who will you serve? How will you find them?
- What will be required for launch?
- How much money will be required for launch?
- Who will help you with the launch?
- How will this company look in six months? One year? Five years?

CHOOSING THE RIGHT BUSINESS

Some of the things I like to look at when selecting the business I will be involved in include the following:

The nature of the problem I am solving. What is the real problem the business solves? I am not necessarily saying that I am searching for a big and important problem here. Sometimes I am just looking for a problem to solve that I find interesting. Part of this involves determining if there are people who would also agree that this problem needs to be solved. People vote with their wallets on what they find valuable. If the problem is only important to you, it will be difficult to become profitable.

My skill sets. While I know that I will eventually bring in the expertise of others to support this business, I always feel like I want to have some basic knowledge about the marketplace, the products, or the customers whom I will serve.

The assets I already have. When considering a potential business, I like to take a careful look at the assets I already have at my disposal. Who do I already know who can help me?

Foundations sometimes take time and patience. Here are a few things you need and a few reasons why it can take a little longer.

Identity

Launching a company is not just about knowing what you do and who you will serve; it's also about deciding how your company will be perceived by those using your services or products. This is partly a conversation about branding, but it's also about culture. Who will you serve and how will you interact with them? Many entrepreneurs never think about this. They assume that it's not really that important and they will figure it out as they go or that their business's identity will develop automatically. I am going to suggest that you take some time and decide what you want your identity to be in advance. If you decide and then actively create it, you will arrive at what you want rather than what the marketplace decides for you.

Legality

Many of the entrepreneurs I have met over the years have held off on getting the legal elements of their business in order because they think it's too expensive. In most cases, you don't have a business until you have the legal structure set up. Setting up legally is an important step of becoming a real business. I don't want to turn this into a book on legal structures of companies and the benefits and potential liabilities of each form. I would suggest you meet with a lawyer to determine your best options. Most lawyers will allow for a free consultation prior to hiring their services. At this stage, once you have your structure figured out, I suggest you will also want to have agreements made. Your agreements may vary depending on your needs. You may even wish to raise some capital. (Remember what I said earlier in the book about trying to maintain as much ownership of your venture as you can. Keep this in mind as you talk to your lawyer if you need to raise funds.) You will certainly need agreements to have others helping you as either employees, contractors, consultants, virtual assistants, or the like. I would recommend starting with a standard work-for-hire agreement. Your lawyer can help you understand this document.

One of the most important things you will need to do is clarify that you will own anything created for you. Have a clear termination clause that protects you, and a requirement for those who work for you to promptly surrender materials and aid any transfer to a replacement person. I also like to have a non-compete clause where possible. Your lawyer may have some additional ideas.

Bookkeeping and Accounting

Most people wonder why I would include this so early considering there isn't any money yet. The reality is that a good accountant can also help with business structure and save you a lot of money and headache later on. Despite what most new entrepreneurs think, a good accountant isn't an expense but a wise investment. Speaking from experience, don't just hire any accountant. Find one that understands your business and has the skill set to help you. A good accountant can make or break your company.

You can sometimes do the bookkeeping yourself during the very early stages of your company. There is a lot of good and easy-to-use software available. I will invite you to delegate this task fairly soon, however, as taking it on yourself can be very time consuming and isn't really cost effective in the long run. Remember, your goal is written on the cover of this book: the six-minute workday.

Often, your setup can take additional time because the professionals mentioned above can sometimes work a little slower as well. It's important to start recognizing this so that you can make decisions and be prepared for delays accordingly. Generally, rushing this part of your business creates mistakes or unnecessary expenses.

IMPORTANT ACTIVITIES DURING THE CREATION PHASE

There are some activities that I have found extremely useful at this particular stage of creation as well.

Networking

I like to start networking as soon as I can when I am creating a business. It is a great place to find people who can help me with the tasks necessary to build the company. I have also hired great people whom I found through networking and who have helped make the company profitable quickly.

Now, I want to clarify that there are definitely different kinds of networking.

I often don't spend a lot of time networking at the lower-level events. Often, these events are full of other new business owners having lunch or breakfast just trying to find customers for their own companies. These kinds of events haven't really helped me build a six-minute workday. What I am talking about are higher-level events with people who are not there to sell, but rather to network or collaborate. A mentor of mine once said this about the different levels of networking: "You'll never do a million-dollar deal at a ten-dollar breakfast."

As you move up to higher levels of networking, you will find a corresponding higher level of collaboration. You are not looking to sell at this level of networking. You are looking to build relationships and find high-level people. Some of these people will join your team, others will open doors or make introductions on your behalf.

I hope I'm not coming off as too negative toward the small business-to-business-style networking events. They have their place; it's just not in the six-minute workday framework.

Investigating Systems

An essential activity at the creation level of the six-minute workday is to investigate systems that you can bring into your company. Remember, systems are the foundation of leverage, which is exactly what you need in order to gain your time freedom, money freedom, and location freedom. You'll remember that systems entail either delegation, automation, or the use of an existing system.

Don't be in a rush to implement a system or utilize a person on your team without understanding what you need the system to do and then verifying that the system will be able to do it. Oftentimes, people are very good at selling themselves as the solution. Make sure you test and try. Make sure you have agreements that protect you. Make sure you have a safety net in case you need to bring in a better way. I have found a good rule to live by is that no system is permanent (including people). If something or someone isn't working out, then you need to find a replacement or a better way. For a person, that can mean more training or a new position in your organization, but sometimes it means they should be let go.

One of the most valuable things I learned about hiring people came from my friend Howard Putnam, former VP of customer service for United Airlines and the CEO of Southwest Airlines. He encouraged me to hire people for their attitudes first and their abilities second. This advice has been a real blessing in my life. When you hire someone with a good attitude, they are a greater support to your company than a more skilled person with a bad attitude.

It is also important to consider training when you bring on a new person or a new system. It will take time for you to learn a system and also to teach it to others. This is one of the reasons why the creation phase of your six-minute workday can be the longest.

As you are selecting people and training them for various tasks in your company, it is essential that you look for leadership qualities. You'll see as we get to the next phases of maintain and expansion & continuity that you will be looking for leaders. These people will replace you in the job of trainer and motivator for your other team members. I would caution you not to be too hasty in talking about your search for leaders until you have been able to observe people in action for a while. But as soon as you start to see positive patterns, let them know that there is a potential future with your business. You should be on a constant quest for leaders.

Ensuring Consistency and Connection

At this stage, consistently checking in and checking up on tasks and people is essential. Remember that you are training them on how to treat you and establishing your expectations of them.

I have had many experiences in my own businesses creating expectations at this level. At this phase of creation, it is not uncommon for me to connect with the people overseeing my systems several times a day. I make sure they know that I am watching carefully and that I am aware of everything. Since most of my recent work hasn't been in a physical office, it's difficult to directly supervise someone without being in the same room, but I still like to be in touch. There are two primary reasons for this.

Support. Obviously if they know you are nearby, they can immediately ask any questions they have. You don't want someone to feel unsure and thus do nothing. If a person feels supported, they will be dedicated. It's also important in the early stages that they understand your working style, your level of dedication, your expectations, and also your constant interest in the results that are being created. Recently, with one of the personal development movies I released, we worked with a team that was a little relaxed on their approach to marketing and sales. This quickly changed as they realized that I was watching the numbers in real time and becoming concerned when hourly goals weren't met. As I began to reach out to them throughout the day, they could tell I was very aware of what was going on. They stepped up their game and, in some areas, tried to get me answers before they knew I would come looking.

Training. Sometimes it's easy to assume we know what someone else will need to know to be successful. Sometimes we even take for granted that others know as much about something as we do. Even after someone has received an initial round of training, I am a huge advocate of ongoing training. Training is one way to ensure not only that people understand but that they are motivated and operating at a consistent level of quality. Regular training also shows that you care and that you are committed to the success of those supporting you.

I have always found it useful to have a weekly training available to my support teams. Sometimes I have done specialized trainings—for example, for those who are selling our services. And we always have team trainings, too, that involve everyone.

One of your big goals with training is to quickly start including the team members themselves in the creation and execution of training programs, especially as you begin to identify leaders. You can't have a six-minute workday if you are spending the entire day preparing for and conducting trainings. At this stage of creation, you are teaching those who will eventually conduct these trainings how they are to be conducted and what is expected.

One of the essential parts of training that has really served to grow my business is to dedicate a portion of the time to sharing and reporting on goals. Reporting isn't just sharing your "numbers"; it's also about sharing a game plan as to how those numbers will be achieved and asking all members of the team for their suggestions. For my businesses, this has been an extremely valuable way to get the entire team to buy in to our goals and help each other as we strive to achieve them.

Training is often a powerful bonding experience that strengthens the team. It is one of the best ways to accelerate your journey toward a six-minute workday.

SIDE THOUGHT: If you want to dramatically increase productivity and improve motivation and connection in your team, create regular contests. We have weekly contests in many of my companies. These contests are often built to drive collaboration rather than competition. They are designed in such a way that pretty much everyone can win. I prefer to have contests that don't single out one person as the winner, but rather highlight the best efforts of everyone. The prizes you offer need not be expensive—although they could be. One of my friends, Bill Bartmann, used to take a large group of his employees and their families to Disneyland. What's most important is for people who excel to feel recognized and appreciated. There are lots of creative ways to do this.

A final note on the creation phase of your business, and perhaps this concept applies to every phase. Most likely you've heard lots of business gurus and personal development people out there encouraging you to take *massive action*. The idea of massive action seems to be one of the most repeated phrases they have. I am sorry to be the one to tell you this, but they are wrong.

I learned directly from the best businesspeople in the world that they weren't focused on massive action. They don't want you to take action for the sake of getting busy. They want you to take *deliberate action*. Deliberate action—action that is focused and purposeful—is better than massive action.

Make sure that whatever you do has purpose and is drawing you closer to your mission.

QUESTIONS: CREATION: AN ACTIVE BEGINNING

- How can you build a good beginning?
- How will you stay focused as you begin to create?
- What's the real problem you are solving? Do others agree it's a problem worth solving?
- What are your skill sets?
- What assets do you already have that can help you?
- What will your identity be?
- What will your legal structure be?
- Who will be your accountant?
- Where are you networking? Who are you looking to meet at these events?
- How are you training? How often are you training?
- How are you using goal setting in your training sessions to support and motivate your employees?

ACTION STEPS

1. Take some time to separate your good ideas from your best ideas. Remember that you will be working on this idea for a long time. It will become a very dominant part of your life and even your identity. Make sure you select something that you are going to be happy with and feel fulfilled by. Don't just chase something because of its profit potential.

2. When I was first starting in business, I had a mentor use the metaphor of assembling an army for an invasion. He suggested I should take an inventory of all the soldiers I had that could help me. His interpretation of soldiers was all of the talents, tools, assets, contacts, resources, and elements I had access to that would allow me to create a successful business. With this list of "soldiers," I quickly became aware of all of the support I had and my confidence increased dramatically. Having this list also gave me a greater awareness of how I could use all of these "soldiers" in the most strategic way. If you were to assemble your army right now, what would make the list?

3. When it comes to identity, I suggest you look at the current marketplace and observe what identities are

already there. I have never felt that there is a benefit for an entrepreneur to create a company that is a carbon copy of one that already exists and try and serve the same people that the existing company is already serving. Find something that is different, better, or unique in your marketplace. Customers are excited when they are given a choice of which tribe to belong to. Decide now what parts of your identity will differentiate you in the marketplace.

4. Create an organizational chart that includes the positions in your company you will need to fill. These positions will be primarily a reflection of the tell, sell, and service components we spoke about in chapter 4. Once you can see the positions you need to fill, you can now go on a hunt to find these people.

5. Encourage your team to set their own goals for their performance. Often when a person is assigned a goal, they don't feel ownership of it. Sometimes they may even doubt the goal and it begins to feel more like a quota. When team members are involved in setting their own goals, they feel a sense of personal responsibility and connection that makes them more committed.

CHAPTER AHA MOMENTS

- How you start determines much of how you will continue.
- Look for more than just profit potential in your business ideas.
- People vote with their wallets on what they find valuable.
- From the beginning, protect yourself legally.
- Be on a constant quest for leaders.
- Make sure that whatever you do has purpose and is drawing you closer to your mission.

Chapter 7

PHASE 2–MAINTENANCE: KEYS TO KEEPING THINGS INTACT

My definition of maintenance is a little different from what you might find in the dictionary. The dictionary definition has a lot to do with becoming and staying satisfied or keeping a result consistent. This might be a useful description for other scenarios but it doesn't work for business in the long term. Maintenance in business isn't just about maintaining the status quo or keeping things consistent with what you have done before.

In business we must recognize that maintenance requires staying relevant as well. We must be aware and open to innovations in the marketplace and shifts that may require us to pivot. We have certainly seen clear examples of this necessity during the COVID-19 pandemic, but realistically you need to be innovating all the time and not waiting for an emergency to force you in that direction.

Innovation doesn't just mean improving the products and systems you are using. Innovation requires you to look at every aspect of your business and make efforts to improve in all ways and in all areas.

I was once asked what the hardest thing for most entrepreneurs is when it comes to innovation and the concept of maintenance in their business. The biggest challenge I see for most entrepreneurs is keeping things simple or making them even more simple. The grand goal of Phase 2: Maintain is—simplify.

Leonardo da Vinci once said that "simplicity is the ultimate sophistication." This is true for most entrepreneurs, many of whom are busy bodies and, for the most part, feel somewhat useless unless they are tinkering with their business. Often, however, their puttering makes things more chaotic or complex. The concept of simplicity is at the very heart of the six-minute workday.

Your goal is to simplify every aspect of your business. As you do this, you will experience greater success and ease. Your customers will see more clearly, your team will know exactly what to do and be able to train each other more easily, and everything will simply flow.

In this phase of your business, you need to learn how to measure and test. Anything that can be improved must be tested. Identifying anything that is complicated and could be simplified is also a must.

WHERE AND HOW TO SIMPLIFY

For many entrepreneurs who are primarily creators, simplifying is a difficult responsibility. Measurement, testing, and adjustments are not skills that come naturally to most, but there are many reasons why they are valuable to learn. There are the obvious reasons of increasing profit, understanding customer behavior, and being able to predict trends. But more than these basic reasons, we also need to learn how to be more effective to save costs, simplify and speed up systems, and predict and solve problems before they appear.

There are many things you should measure to ensure your companies' growth and survival. If you want to graduate to a six-minute workday, there are even more things you'll want to measure. You will also have to teach your team to measure and report on these things. We will divide these into two categories of essentials:

- Essential numbers
- Essential activities

Essential Numbers

Peter Drucker once said, "If it isn't measured, it can't improve." If you want to maintain and grow your business, you have to keep an eye on essential numbers. Essential numbers are the targeted specific numbers that you will want reported back to you. These could include such things as sales figures (I like to collect mine at least once daily), leads generated, amount spent on advertising, conversion figures if they are available, expenses and costs, average spend per customer, cost of acquisition of customers, and so forth. You can get a complete chart and some sample reports of what I ask my teams for each day at www.SixMinuteWorkday.com.

Watching essential numbers is like looking at the fruit in a tree. The fruit has already arrived and sometimes it can be a little late or less than expected. However, you often identify trends and approaching challenges by having these numbers. On the flip side of this coin—when things are going well, they can be indicators of a trend that is arriving.

In my companies, I receive some of these numbers through a portal that gives me a reflection in real time. I can check any time, twenty-four hours a day, and it reflects exactly what the numbers are minute by minute. This has been very valuable for tracking things in real time. For example, with one of the movies I recently released, I am able to go into our reporting and I can see how often the sales of that film are occurring. There have been a few times when I have seen abnormally long pauses between sales, and this prompts me to reach out to members of my team and get answers as to why we are having that problem. More than a few times we have discovered technological challenges that, had I not been able to monitor these essential numbers, might have gone unobserved for days.

Even though I am now easily managing a six-minute workday, I still like to check several times a day. Each check takes literally seconds. But there is great peace of mind in knowing that things are on track.

An analogy I often like to share is that measurement is a little like flying an airplane on an international flight. There is great comfort in knowing you're heading in the right direction. And just like with the airplane analogy, if things are not quite right you can make small adjustments pretty quickly to remain on course. I am so thankful for technology that allows for quick observations and immediate corrections where necessary.

Essential Activities

While the essential numbers are like looking at the fruit in a tree, essential activities are more like looking at the roots of the tree. These activities can often indicate what the numbers will reflect in the near or distant future.

Some of the essential activities I like to monitor are the number of customers contacted, hours spent in specific activities in the day, and a description of activities and progress reports that show where my key people are spending their time.

Most of these reports are given to me each day; however, I don't review these in detail as they often take a little more time, and I trust those I've put in leadership roles to handle these reports. One of the things I am going to encourage you to start doing in the maintenance and improvement phase of the six-minute workday is to move some of your most trusted people into leadership and management roles.

EMPOWERING LEADERSHIP

Let's talk about leaders and people for a moment. The wonderful thing about technology and automation systems is that they do exactly what they've been programmed to do. You can count on it. People, on the other hand, function quite differently. Sometimes they start well and then go off course. Sometimes they start slow and get better. There is a level of unpredictability when you are dealing with people.

One of the best ways to start regulating the productivity and predictability of people is to train them in the correct principles of delegation. Delegation is basically empowering someone else to do a job or task on your behalf.

There are a lot of really great tools available that can teach you the skills of effective delegation. But I'd like to share some basics so that if you're unfamiliar with some of these techniques you can still get started right away without having to go buy another book.

Clarity

The first step of delegation is to clearly set out what you want done and establish some boundaries around how you expect it to be accomplished. Defining the outcome that you expect is one of the most important parts of delegation. Generally, when I find people failing at a task that has been delegated to them, it is rarely for a lack of desire or a lack of trying. Often it is because the desired approach and outcome hasn't been made clear to the person completing the task. They don't know exactly what to do and they become afraid that they might make a mistake. As a result, they do nothing. You need to make absolutely sure that they understand the task and how it leads to the ultimate outcome.

In addition to sharing your expectations of the result, you need to be clear about when you want the job done and any other specific details that are relevant to the task. For example, I recently delegated a task and I needed to specify who could help get it done with this person so they wouldn't take other team members from an important meeting.

Boundaries

When I delegate a task to someone, I don't like to give too many rules as to how they can arrive at the desired outcome. I want the individual to be able to use their talents, creativity, and resources to reach the end result. Often, I will set up some simple parameters and boundaries just to ensure they are operating in a way that doesn't jeopardize the reputation of the company and that we maintain our integrity. Other than that, I don't give too many rules.

Reporting Back

In business there is a principle known as Pearson's Law, attributed to statistician Karl Pearson. It states: "When performance is measured, performance improves. When performance is measured and reported back, the rate of improvement accelerates." If you want to see improvement, you need to be clear that you are expecting a report back regarding the task that has been delegated. I also like to clarify the method of the report and with whom the report should be shared. When people know that a report is expected, they always perform better than if they feel like you'll simply forget about it.

Opportunity for Failure

Something that is not talked about that often when it comes to the art of delegation is the concept of failure. Now, I have to be honest. I don't come out and tell the people I am assigning a task to: "You probably will fail, and that's okay." Instead, I assure them that I have full confidence in their ability to do this or solve this challenge, and I further assure them that if they encounter challenges or difficulties that I am there to support them. Most of the time when I frame things in this way, people do just fine and I never hear from them until they give a report of completion.

When delegating, I think it's important to have confidence that the individual will be successful. I have often been surprised that the person has actually discovered a better way to do things than I had at first supposed.

Sometimes I hear of entrepreneurs who are afraid to delegate to others because they feel like there will be big mistakes made. Unless you learn to delegate effectively, you will never be able to attain a six-minute workday. Delegation is an essential skill.

So, what can you do if you have this fear of delegation leading to big mistakes? The best advice I've received was to simply look first at myself. How often do I get things perfect? Never. How often do I get it pretty well? Probably about 70 to 80 percent of the time. Realistically this will be what you can expect in terms of performance from others. They will most likely get it right about as often as you do if you teach and train them well.

One of my mentors pointed out that people will also get better as you trust them more to figure things out. In a very short period of time, they will most likely exceed your 70 to 80 percent of effectiveness. But you have got to give them space up front to make some mistakes. Consider it a required part of your business journey.

For those of you still holding onto this fear, I have to confess that while I have seen some small mistakes along the way, I never experienced someone make a mistake so bad that it destroyed my company. Most of the mistakes were easily fixed and didn't interrupt business or even disrupt profits. If you hire right and get people who are there to help, there is very little that can go wrong.

Delegating doesn't need to be a onetime event or task. In fact, often it works best when it is a long-term, ongoing responsibility because that person who takes on the responsibility gets better at it and develops the talents and skills to complete the task more quickly and efficiently.

Before we leave this conversation on delegation, I want to point out that during this phase you need to be looking for more and more opportunities to delegate. The more responsibility you can share, the faster you will arrive at your six-minute workday. Having said that, you must take each instance of delegation seriously. It can't be rushed and you shouldn't take these moments for granted.

One of the top achievers I interviewed shared an interesting insight on delegation. Each quarter, he makes a list of all the things that he is still doing. He gives each item a value or a cost—a measurement in two numbers. The first assesses how important a task is and the second estimates what it would cost him to get someone else to do it. This allows him to focus his efforts and time on the projects and freedoms he wants to enjoy. He literally delegates almost every activity he doesn't want to do.

Obviously, your profits, growth, and your ability to delegate are connected. Be sure that you delegate as you grow instead of trying to give everything away as quickly as you can. My advice is to give tasks to others as they and the company develop the maturity to support the task going to another person. Remember always that no one will ever care about your company as much as you do.

A Warning on Handling Mistakes

I was a little hesitant to share this last one but then I got an email from one of my one-on-one entrepreneur coaching students that made me think others would find it helpful too. In the email he expressed incredible frustration with a situation that one of his team members had created. He genuinely felt bad and confessed that perhaps he may have lost his temper. As he explained the situation, I could tell why he was frustrated, but I also felt his sincerity in feeling bad about losing his cool.

As I think back to the interviews I did with the top entrepreneurs, I remember a few of them sharing their most challenging moments. Obviously, when looking back, they had more composure about it than in the moment when it occurred. But one thing they did mention consistently is that you need to be careful about getting too emotional publicly when things go wrong and be very careful about what one of these mentors called "having a public execution."

While sometimes a "public execution" is valuable—such as in cases of theft, dishonesty, or extreme disloyalty—the majority of the time a private conversation after a little time has passed is best. I try to make it a personal rule to never embark on a mission to correct a mistake until I can explain with clarity what has happened.

On that note . . .

WHAT ABOUT USING VAs (VIRTUAL ASSISTANTS)?

I have seen an explosive shift toward the use of virtual assistants in recent years. I think they are great for certain tasks but terrible for others. They definitely have their place in business in modern times. But I want to share a few thoughts.

I know there have been some popular books and gurus who show how you can use virtual assistants to create your laptop lifestyle. I would agree for that end result they are a perfect resource. But there is a difference between creating a lifestyle of a few hundred thousand dollars and living like a king in Bali or Thailand for a few years. If that is your goal, then you will have no problem getting a VA to help you part-time.

But if your goal is to build something larger and more permanent, you have to focus on leadership over lifestyle. You need to be looking at people who are going to be able to move into more permanent positions with your team.

In short, you will have to find people who can become your managers. These people will need to be committed enough that they will stick with you through all phases of the six-minute workday and beyond. These people are going to need to have the qualities of a loyal steward and you will have to reward them accordingly.

My experience has been that while VAs are earnest and really do try hard, they often have difficulty dedicating themselves to just one client. In fact, while I have some pretty good VAs, I have typically found that as they get more and more clients (which is what they are always searching for) everyone using that VA suffers. If you have the ability to hire someone under an exclusivity contract, do it.

And naturally, every time you need to replace a virtual assistant, you also need to retrain a new person. This is one of the reasons why you can never really build a million-dollar or multimillion-dollar venture, and definitely not a six-minute workday, with a virtual assistant. The use of virtual assistants in prime company roles leads to a constant state of recruitment, replacement, and training.

COMPENSATION TO YOUR SUPPORT TEAM

Compensation is a difficult conversation because you will ultimately have to determine a person's worth by what they are able to bring to your organization. I am an advocate of paying people well. This keeps them committed and enthusiastic. It also keeps them focused on helping you create success and keeps them from looking for a side hustle of their own or another opportunity elsewhere. Just keep in mind that this is where you have to be a smart entrepreneur and budget effectively so you are not sending all of your profits out the door.

I am an advocate of some element of profit participation or performance pay. Often, this gets people more excited to give their best and be a team player. If there is profit participation across the entire team, you'll find that team members help one another to reach their goals.

For those who are in temporary positions to help you or work-for-hire–type positions, remember that everything is negotiable. Be careful not to overpay or over-commit. Especially if you have never had an experience working with this group or individual before. I have made it a rule of thumb to never pay the full fee up-front when working with new individuals.

I generally will take the full invoice and divide it by three, paying the first third at the start of the agreement, the second third when 50 percent of the work is complete, and the final third upon completion and approval of the finished work.

When working with a third party, it is a good idea to have your lawyer draft or review a contract before commencing the work.

GET YOUR FLOW

No doubt things are starting to get exciting as you start adding some team members and you are beginning to see your time freedom return. At this point I start to see some entrepreneurs experience a little difficulty, even though they often don't see this difficulty themselves. What they see is the six-minute workday entering into sight, so they start trying to grow to the next phase too quickly.

Make this your mantra: Get the flow before you grow.

What do I mean by this? I mean take some time during this phase to make sure your company is running smoothly. Make sure that everybody knows their job and feels confident and comfortable doing it. Make sure everybody is becoming comfortable performing their work without direct supervision. You'll soon see at this stage who among your employees are your self-starters and potential leaders.

QUESTIONS: PHASE 2–MAINTENANCE: KEYS TO KEEPING THINGS INTACT

- What is your definition of maintenance?
- What are you doing to continually innovate in your business?
- What are you measuring?
- How are you receiving reports of your essential numbers?
- How often are you receiving reports?
- What can you delegate?
- How are your delegation skills?
- Do you have a strategy for correcting mistakes and coaching someone after they've made a mistake?
- Where can you use a virtual assistant in your company, and where will you need a permanent person?
- How are you compensating your team?

ACTION STEPS

1. Create a standardized report that your team can use to share essential numbers. Standardizing the report will allow you to quickly find the information you are looking for. Having a standard reporting template unifies everyone and saves time. Your team will also grow in the habit of understanding what is important

to measure and where their focus should be. On occasion you may want to add or request specific reports that may be outside of the norm.

2. Even when you get into the six-minute-workday level of your business, you should check your numbers regularly, so get into the habit of doing so now. If you build the standardized reports, you can check them from anywhere and it doesn't take long. The strangest places I have checked my numbers include hanging upside down on a ride at an amusement park, on a boat heading out to go scuba diving, and quickly at a school Christmas concert. I generally won't check when I'm with my family, but if you know how to read your numbers quickly, it literally takes just seconds. In fact, I love the feeling of seeing that I am actually experiencing positive results in my business when I am enjoying my time doing other activities. It is a real sense of accomplishment when you are doing just fine while having the freedom to be elsewhere.

3. On another note: Quick and regular checks give you the ability to get things back on track quickly if something goes wrong. Remember that you are not going to do this—you have a team for this.

4. Take some time and think about how you want to compensate those you will bring in as your support. Remember always that you definitely don't want to share ownership or control. You are not looking for

partners; you are looking for support on the creation of transactions. Consider that you always want to be generous with your compensation or people will go elsewhere or, worse, to your competitors.

CHAPTER AHA MOMENTS

- Innovation is an essential activity in business.
- Simplify.
- Constant regular reporting helps you keep things on track.
- No one will ever care about your company as much as you do.
- When you are growing your team, look for leaders and people who are committed to your mission.
- Correct mistakes with clarity.
- Compensate those you work with well and they will be loyal.
- Get the flow before you grow.

Chapter 8

PHASE 3–EXPANSION AND CONTINUITY

The goal of every entrepreneur I have ever spoken with includes the idea of expanding their ideas and concepts to serve and impact more people. I have never met a single entrepreneur who has been satisfied with creating something small.

Most likely you feel the same way.

The third phase of the six-minute workday is all about expanding, and there are several things you should do or continue doing at this point in your business.

WORK *ON* YOUR BUSINESS RATHER THAN *IN* IT

Expansion always starts from within. If you want to grow bigger as a company, you are required to grow larger as an individual. You will have to become a better and more competent manager. And if you are not yet enjoying a six-minute workday with a strong team doing most of the heavy lifting, you need to get that sorted out first.

Business is kind of like the toy Lego. You can't build a tall tower until you have a firm foundation. Continue to learn all you can about your business and how to support the people you have helping you run it.

Although I'm presenting the idea of a six-minute workday, that doesn't mean you should ignore thinking about your business at other times. This is what it really means to work *on* your business instead of *in* your business. You have support in place now so you don't have to be in attendance for every activity.

And you'd be surprised where you can do your thinking and planning around your business. I have had brilliant business ideas while sitting in a penthouse swimming pool in Manila in the Philippines. I once had an idea on how to help one of my team members perform better while scuba diving in the Caribbean. I remember bringing a notebook to the edge of an infinity pool in Mexico. I also had a really good idea once hit me while in line for the Haunted Mansion at Disneyland. Again, this thinking about my business didn't take much time, but I allow inspiration to hit when it decides. (And, personally, I find inspiration for my business comes much easier when I am relaxed and enjoying my life.)

Tavin always thought that a business would only thrive if he gave long hours and full days to it. It took a lot for him to trust the idea that others could do a lot of the heavy lifting in his company for him. He had not had less than a sixteen-hour workday, let alone a six-minute one. We convinced him to join us on of one our cruises to the tropics. That meant he had to trust his team and unplug. It was while there that he had the realization that they could make just as much money without him and that everything was fine without his direct, minute-by-minute involvement.

One day during the cruise, I came into the spa on the ship and found him taking notes furiously in the sauna. As I came in, he couldn't contain his excitement. He confessed he finally knew what it meant to work on *his business rather than* in *it. While relaxing, he saw clearly exactly what he needed to get his team doing to tap into a new market for his company. I don't think I ever saw him so excited. And he credited it all to stepping out of his company and putting himself in a zone where he was able to receive inspiration.*

EXPAND YOUR NETWORK

Part of expanding who you are is connected to who you spend time with. I encourage you to join high-level networking associations and clubs. Spend time with other leaders. Learn from them, play with them, and observe how they solve problems and your answers will also come. You've heard it said that your network equals your net worth. This is very true. But I have found that before your network can become your net worth, your network must become your safety net. In other words, your peers are going to help you with everything from your minor questions and beliefs about yourself to helping you find opportunities and connections you may not have had previously.

If you are unsure of how to level up your network, reach out to me and I will share with you how to come hang out with our tribe. My tribe includes many of the top entrepreneurs I have spoken about throughout this book. We do mastermind retreats and cruises in exotic locations. There is a strong spirit of collaboration and big deals often get done.

A few years ago, Josh and his business partner, Dan, from Vancouver came on one of our cruises. We left from Houston and visited ports like Belize, Cozumel, and Roatán. But as we boarded the ship, before we even left the port, they closed a deal that allowed them to raise three million dollars as they collaborated with others in our tribe. I think that was the fastest deal on one of our cruises.

There is massive power in the network you spend time with.

REMAIN ON THE HUNT FOR GOOD PEOPLE

One of the top entrepreneurs I interviewed once told me, "You are always in the people business. Every business is a people business. And it's not just about the customers. It's also about your support team." While in expansion mode, you must always remain on the hunt for great people to support your existing or expanding opportunities.

The quest to find the best people to help you will continue for as long as you operate your enterprises. Regardless of how long you have been in business, you will find that people leave or need to be replaced for one reason or another.

Keep looking for good people.

ALWAYS BE TRAINING

Training is the key to developing good people and keeping them motivated. Everyone wants to feel like they are making progress. The good news is that you don't have to be the one to create or provide the training. Much of this can now come from those you've placed in leadership roles. In fact, many of these people will feel privileged or honored to know that you respect them enough to ask them to lead the development of others at the company.

As you give these rising stars training and leadership opportunities, make sure they understand the importance of being consistent, supportive, and aware of the true needs of your people. Often, new leaders need a little supervision at first just to help them understand the nature of their assignment.

In my experience you are best off finding people who have a proven track record of success, being helpful, and serving others. Take the time to confirm their loyalty and capabilities. I have never had a person morph into an egotistical power monster when given a leadership position.

And, naturally, as people move into a leadership role, be sure to consider a compensation increase.

REPLACE YOURSELF

Your primary goal during both the maintenance and expansion phases of the six-minute workday is really to replace yourself. Remember that you are not looking for the perfect person to do so. You are looking for a competent person whom you can trust to do a good job and keep the venture profitable. You do this by finding good people and then continuing to train them and help them feel connected and committed to the organization. People often go rogue when they are left alone.

So, when you replace yourself, you need to find people who are good managers and leaders. They need to understand the importance of keeping people connected and producing as a team. Once you have replaced yourself, the regularity of reporting and staying close to your leaders will ensure that things continue to run in good order.

ESTABLISH REGULAR REPORTING

At this phase you still need regular reporting. In fact, for me, the bulk of the 360 seconds of my workday is spent reviewing the brief reports I get daily. The way my reports are structured, I can usually be finished and respond back to the leader who created the report within fifteen seconds once I have understood the report.

I would invite you to plan for a longer session with them from time to time to review and plan with your bigger goals in mind. I generally conduct about a fifteen-minute planning session with each of my core leaders once a month or as needed. When a new project comes up or bigger clients get involved, you may have to spend a little extra time.

I also have a relatively open-door policy where I invite people other than leaders to approach me with concerns or questions. Rarely do I hear from them because most of the time the leaders I choose have really good relationships with those they are working with. But from time to time I will get a question that I can generally handle quickly or delegate back to the leader. (Remember that even how you respond is a form of training.)

SO WHAT ABOUT ADDING ANOTHER VENTURE?

Now that your initial venture has enough momentum and strong enough roots, adding another venture may be something you consider. If this is you, then keep in mind you will be starting again at the beginning with the creation phase. You will not be receiving a six-minute workday yet. But before you rush back to the creation chapter, I want you to consider what expansion really looks like and some ways to start either expanding your current operations or adding to them. You might find a better decision will be to expand your current venture rather than adding a new one.

INVEST

Instead of building a whole new business venture, one of the things I have added to my income streams is the pillar of investing—getting your money to work for you. I have personal investments and my companies also have their own investments. Naturally, there are tax benefits involved with how we invest, but there are also many other significant benefits.

For example, an investment one of my companies makes is in a Real Estate Income Trust (REIT). (As this isn't an investment book, I invite you to google "REIT" to learn more about how they work.) This particular REIT pays a cashflow dividend every month. I have used this money to expand my company or, if I don't need to, I simply reinvest it to keep that cash growing. One of the things that has been really helpful by doing this is that the company develops significant cash reserves. At any given time shifts in the marketplace may put some stress on the business. If you've got cash reserves, that stress is less.

One important note is that these cash reserves should be easily available if you need them and they need to be highly secure. Don't worry about getting a massive return on your money by making a risky unsecured investment. Think slow, steady, and accessible if needed.

Just as with everything else in the six-minute workday, you want to try to make contributions automatic and easy. What I have done is simply create an automatic transfer of funds into an investment of choice. These transfer amounts are altered as needed to make sure the business continues to run smoothly. And the reserves aren't something I redeem unless required. The goal is to build the reserves, not use them as you would a delay bank account.

By now you may notice some patterns in your business. One pattern I have noticed is that there are certain seasons during which we are extremely busy and others when we are not. These cash reserves also help to weather those periods of scarcity.

Carla from Idaho really struggled with instability in her business. This created all kinds of challenges with cashflow and consistency. She had developed a pretty good structure and she could manage her business in about an hour a day. With a few tweaks she would be closer to a six-minute workday. But this cashflow thing really had her worried. How could she afford to make the jump to the support she needed when there was such unpredictability in her business?

It was then that she began to identify patterns. Hers were specifically that around Christmastime and in the summer business was slow. At other times of the year, her company thrived and did really well. Her peak period, she discovered, was April/May. As she used the principle of patterns and cash reserves, she was able to build a more consistent and predictable flow. She put money into investments that provide constant cashflow, but she made arrangements to only receive the cashflow injections in the slow periods of the year. As a result, she was able to make the jump to a shorter workday and experience greater growth even during the slow months.

QUESTIONS: EXPANSION AND CONTINUITY

- Who else can you find to help you expand?
- How are you building your network?
- How are you finding great people to join your team?
- How are you continuing to train your team?

- How do you know if you are ready to launch a second venture?
- How are you building cash reserves to utilize when potential challenges arise?
- What patterns does your business follow—which are the best times and when is business slow?

ACTION STEPS

1. Find associations, clubs, and networking groups you can join to expand your network. Leaders learn from other leaders. And if you want to become a leader, you must surround yourself with other leaders. There are lots of amazing groups out there that can help you create success beyond your wildest dreams. Don't be afraid to invest in becoming part of these groups. And then, when you do join them, take a leadership role through which you can get really involved. (We have a list of several great organizations on www .SixMinuteWorkday.com.)

2. As you replace yourself more and more, you will need leaders who are self-starters, well organized, good at keeping people connected and contributing, and good reporters. You will want to keep in touch with these leaders daily, even if it is by text or other short communications. They need to know most of all that

you are committed to their success. They need to have the same vision as you do for the company.

3. If you are thinking about launching a second venture, take some time to carefully prepare. Don't rush into a new venture until you are confident that you are able to give it the time and resources necessary to make it successful. Too many entrepreneurs lose focus and money when they split themselves between two or more ventures. Make sure that your initial venture is self-sustaining and requires little attention from you. Sometimes it is best to just expand what you are currently doing than to start something new. Decide which move is right for you.

4. When building a cash reserve for your company, it is a good idea to meet with a few different financial planners to get some ideas around what options you have. Each organization with financial planners has a variety of products available to help you. Some of these might be better for your needs than others. For my personal life, I look at long-term growth and consistency. I let my company pay my living expenses, so I generally never have to touch any of these accumulating investments. The strategy for my company, however, is a little different. I take a shorter-term approach and want to make sure I can have access to cash if I need it. Each year, I revisit the patterns of my business and how cashflow has worked

out. If there is a large surplus of funds in my business cash reserves, at that point I will then shift the excess portion to a longer-term venture.

Again, you will have to do some due diligence and a little experimentation over time to see what works best for you personally and for your company. But as one of my mentors told me, "It is wise to invest, but never bite off more than you can chew." In others words, don't stretch the company too far to build a cash reserve. Invest smaller, safer amounts and do it consistently.

CHAPTER AHA MOMENTS

- To expand what you have, you must expand who you are.
- Your network is your safety net.
- A second venture that is similar to or associated with your current venture increases your chances of success.
- Your goal is to replace yourself.
- People go rogue when left alone.
- How you respond to queries from employees is a form of training.
- Look for patterns of prosperity in your business.
- Inspiration comes when you step away from regular activity.

Chapter 9

REPAIR AND RESCUE

This is the chapter that hopefully you don't have to read that often or even ever. Proper creation and maintenance should build your venture in such a way that you never have to worry about repair. But if you do run into trouble, not all is lost.

As I mentioned earlier, I have made the mistake once in my ventures where a significant series of repairs became necessary. At the time, I didn't really know what to do. Thank goodness I was still very connected to many of the multi-millionaire mentors I had interviewed. I decided the quickest way to get this sorted out was to ask for help.

Yes, I felt embarrassed to ask for help at first because I knew that the current challenges had come as a result of my personal neglect. But I was desperate. I was about to lose what I had worked so hard to create. And to be honest, I was also desperately trying to keep the income stream that had given me so much freedom previously.

THE 7 STEPS TO REPAIR AND RESCUE

There is a saying I heard once that, "Older eyes see better." And it's true: people with more experience can often see things that those with younger, inexperienced eyes can't see. This was certainly the case in my situation. After explaining the problems I was encountering to my older millionaire friend, he asked a few questions and then said there are seven steps you need to do to fix things.

1. *Identify What Is Really Happening*

   My mentor told me about how he grew up on a farm and that, when he was a teenager, he was in charge of some goats. Somehow, one of them got out of the pen and wandered off, getting caught in a mess of barbed wire.

   By the time he found the goat, she was pretty tangled up and scraped up too. His first instinct was to just pull the goat out of the mess by her hind legs. But on closer examination he realized that the goat had twisted herself into the mess very tightly. Pulling her out would just cause the barbs to sink deeper into her skin. As he examined how the wire was wrapped around her, he realized that his first job was to get the goat to be still and start cutting away the wire that was wrapped around her belly. Slowly he cut it away and soon had the goat freed enough to pick her up and get her out.

While the first instinct to pull her out may not have killed her, it would have seriously injured her. It's always best to pause and see what's really happening before jumping into action.

As you approach your business to begin repairs, you will need to look carefully as well. This will allow you to get to work in the most effective way and avoid making the problem worse. Sometimes the best solution is to do less or even nothing.

2. *Stop the Bleeding*

Once you know what's going on, you need to stop the bleeding in the best way possible. Stopping the bleeding means to discontinue the areas that are causing you the most loss. In repairing my company, one of the things I needed to do to stop the bleeding was to reach out to my existing customers and get them back on their services. I also had to refund some of them and get them back with one of our team members to resolve their difficulties. Most often when stopping the bleeding, the first place you should start is with your customers. You will need

to make sure they are okay before you make repairs
elsewhere.

3. *Go Back to the Original Transaction*
   Once you have stopped the bleeding, you need to return
   to the construction of your original transaction. This
   is your business in its simplest form. By returning to
   these basics, you can see what is diluting this original
   transaction or preventing it from taking place. When
   you have clarity about your original transaction, then
   you can disassemble and see how each of the individual
   pieces of your business is working to create the current
   circumstances.

*Nelson found this return to the original transaction to be
the most valuable step for him. As his company exploded, he
thought nothing could stop him. He had attempted to grab
bigger market share by adding more people as quickly as he
could to his company. As the new expenses began to catch
up to the barely increasing sales, he knew he had a problem.
As he returned to the original transaction and all the steps
that needed to occur in order for the transaction to happen,
he noticed that he had allowed lots of new and unnecessary
complications to enter into his business. The expenses of these
new, unimportant steps were killing him. He realized that he
put them in to satisfy his ego rather than build his business.
He quickly made the repair, repositioned the efforts of some*

of his key people (downsizing a few), and saw both his profits and his market share grow.

4. *Identify What Led to the Challenge*
   It isn't enough to stop at identifying the challenge. You need to find out what created the challenge. In my case, my own neglect was the root cause, but there were many steps toward improvement that happened as a result. Tracking down the incidents that led to these challenges has actually been very helpful in the repair process. As I began to repair, I have now been able to restore my business and build it stronger than it ever was before.

   Interestingly enough, this has also made me a better teacher of the six-minute workday, as I now know more about what other entrepreneurs might encounter if they follow the same road I did. I have also been able to build several safeguards into my own company to ensure that this never happens again.

5. *Decide if the Problem Can Be Fixed or if You Need to Pivot*
   Some problems take too much effort, time, and expense to fix. Sometimes the effort just isn't worth it. And sometimes your customers don't really care. Sometimes it's just easier to pivot and leave the dead carcass of the past on the trail.

   If you decide that a pivot is required, let me just give you a little advice: be sure to involve your customers in the pivot. It's always better to ask someone what they need before you give it to them. If you want them to buy it, get their opinions on creating it. Always listen to your customers. It is their opinion that matters most.

6. *Determine the Best Way to Fix It*

When I refer to the best way to fix something, I am not talking about the cheapest way. Sometimes the best solution can be very expensive. When I say the best way to fix a problem, I am referring to the most effective and long-lasting way.

Sometimes the most effective solution will require more money, more time, hiring a new resource, or even deconstructing a system you have been using for years.

Sometimes, because the remedy can involve new systems and infrastructures, the repair can actually give you marketplace advantages and improve your business in ways that you've never experienced before. For these reasons and more, I caution you to really look at making the best repairs, not the quickest. Sometimes the best renovations mean knocking down old ways and spending a little bit of money. That said, I do recommend that, whenever possible, you stay open for business during the renovations. Starting from zero is always harder than asking for forgiveness after a few hiccups and modifications. When you can explain changes as an effort to make improvements that will better serve your customers, they are generally excited and willing to support you during the process.

7. *Ask What You Can Do Right Now*
   One of the most important things about the principle of repair is to get started. I have seen too many people decide that, rather than repair, they just need to move into a state of research. Typically, this approach turns out to be an excuse not to take action and has nothing to do with research.

   It's pretty easy if you find yourself in a state of repair to lose confidence and second-guess yourself as you come back to the business. If you fall off your horse, climb back up. You need to get right back on with business. There is no benefit to holding on tight and waiting. And if you are sincere about the idea of doing research, then start the repair and do the research along the way.

Don't worry about making perfect repairs. Focus on getting things back to functional as quickly as you can. Take a look around you and realize that every business is in a constant state of development. In some ways, that's where you will always be. Being in repair mode is just an intense mode of development.

Take a look at any technology product and you see a version 1.0, 2.0, 3.0, and so forth. As I write this, I believe we are on iPhone version 13. Get started and don't worry about being perfect.

I was chatting with one of the partners who created Kajabi recently and he validated everything I said about not waiting for perfection. One of the conclusions we came up with was that it is better to release something 70 percent finished and functional than to wait to come out with something 100 percent ready.

Greg was continually holding back and going back to the drawing board to make things better for his business. Or so he thought. The reality was that he was worried that if he went to market too soon, people would think he didn't know what he was doing or that he was unprofessional. Every time people would ask him about his company, they would get excited and tell Greg that they would definitely use his services. He would then shift gears and talk about the new improvements on the way.

Realizing that they couldn't do business with Greg yet, those he spoke with would often shrug and simply say, "Keep in touch." At the point of hopelessness and out of cash, Greg attended one of my seminars. He realized that, unless he launched soon, he might never get the chance. He launched even though he thought his business was less than 100 percent ready. In truth, he was probably about 60 to 70 percent ready compared to what he wanted. But launch he did and the response was startling. He was an instant success, and those he served never mentioned what was missing.

Over the next year, Greg now had the resources to add to his company and get the original intended changes added. And you'll never guess what happened—long before getting everything finished, he discovered more changes that he needed to make. He realized then that his company would always be in a state of development.

Beware of Overcorrection

When making repairs, it can be easy to go beyond the mark. I have seen several entrepreneurs make this mistake and ultimately it has brought them right back into the business full-time. Correct what you need to and get your team back up and running as quickly as you can. That's the goal.

QUESTIONS: REPAIR AND RESCUE

- Is the problem you've identified truly the real problem?
- What problems led to the challenge?
- Does this issue require a repair or a pivot?
- Are you involving your customers in bigger changes?
- What can you do right now to start repairing?
- What excuses do you hide behind to keep you from getting back into business?

ACTION STEPS

1. Don't think that you need to repair every problem. Sometimes the best thing for you to do is leave the mistake alone and pivot in a new direction.

2. Get started on making your repairs now and don't wait. Sometimes when an entrepreneur's business has serious difficulties and needs repair, it can cause them to lose confidence. Don't let these setbacks knock the wind out of your sails. Pick yourself up and get started.

3. Don't feel like your repairs need to be implemented by you, by yourself. Sometimes your best solutions will come from your team or your customers. Think of your business like a car pulling into the pit at a NASCAR race. Get your team working on the repairs and you'll find that you can get back on the track much quicker.

CHAPTER AHA MOMENTS

- Start by getting a second set of eyes.
- Don't ever be embarrassed to ask for help.
- Make sure the problem you are addressing is truly the real problem.

- Everything important to your business is found back in the original transaction.
- Not everything needs to be fixed.
- Involve your customers in the more significant changes.
- Seventy percent of something is better than 100 percent of nothing.
- Businesses are always in a state of development.
- Every business faces challenges.

Chapter 10

WHAT WILL YOU DO NEXT?

Now that you have a bird's-eye view of the six-minute workday principles, what will you do with them? Having taught these principles around the world, I have seen some massive success stories and I have also seen people who didn't experience any improvement in their lives. Perhaps you may be wondering, as I do, what accounts for this disparity.

Quite frankly, most of the time, those who succeed and those who do not have a lot in common.

- Both groups have often gotten exactly the same training; some of them were even in the same room.
- Many of them come from a similar background and have exactly the same support structures.

- Many of them have had identical financial resources available.
- Many of them have had really good business ideas.

As I took a hard look at what the difference might be, the answer was actually quite simple. It can be shared as a multistep formula. I encourage you to make a commitment right now that you will follow these steps in the exact way I present them. If you do so, I am confident you will begin to experience success with the six-minute workday.

STEP #1: MAKE A DECISION TO BEGIN

The big thing that holds most people back from success is that they never make a firm decision to get started. It's important to understand the difference between a wish and a decision. Wishes are an abstract intention to receive a result. A decision requires taking precise action to create a result. True decisions don't exist unless there is action attached. What's the action you will take to solidify your decision right now?

STEP# 2: DO 5 EASY THINGS EACH DAY

I have to thank my friend Jack Canfield for this idea. When I included Jack in my first film, *The Opus*, I talked with him about the secrets behind how he and Mark Victor Hansen were able to make the *Chicken Soup for the Soul* books—considered the highest-selling books after the Bible—such big sellers.

Jack told me the key to their success was to do five powerful things each day that brought them closer to the goal. Those things did not have to be massive or expensive, but there had to be a consistency to their efforts. As a result, these things compounded on each other and made a major difference in the end.

STEP #3: GET OTHERS INVOLVED QUICKLY

The faster you can get others involved, supporting you and making you accountable, the faster you will likely experience success. When you have others supporting you, you will be surprised at how easily things begin to come together. This principle has been so powerful for me as I have built out my first business that it is now a cornerstone of everything I do. When you go alone, there is risk; when you take friends, you have a massive support network.

STEP #4: DON'T BE AFRAID TO LEARN MORE

Learning is essential for success. Remember that you can't expand what you have until you expand who you are.

STEP #5: BECOME IMMERSED IN THE CONTENT

The deeper you learn, live, and associate with the six-minute-workday principles and others who are living them out, the easier it will be for you to master them in your own life. If a professional athlete tried to master their sport by themselves without teammates, coaches, and opportunities to play at a high level, they wouldn't be able to measure up to their fullest potential. But when you put them with teammates who push them to raise their standards, when you add coaches and trainers who give them drills and new skills to add to their existing talent, that is when they reach their potential.

I would encourage you to get started now and follow these steps. I also invite you to reread this book regularly to allow this content to influence the way you think about your businesses, the way you build your income streams, and the way you value your time.

ADDITIONAL SUCCESS STORIES

The following are some true stories from several of my students over the years who have implemented many of the six-minute-workday strategies that you have now been exposed to. My purpose for sharing these is that I want you to see a few of the different ways these ideas can be used and how you can use them as well.

Obviously, by hearing these success stories, your confidence to implement these principles will also grow. And isn't that what we really want? You want a six-minute workday, and these case studies show that it is possible. And if others have done it and are currently doing it, then why can't you be part of the tribe?

As you experience your own success stories, I invite you to share them with me directly. You can email me personally at doug@douglasvermeeren.com.

Here are a few success stories from some of the people you may meet when you join us at one of our live events.

Keith was a serial entrepreneur. He had tried several different business ventures, and even had several different business coaches and people who wanted to help. However, he had never yet experienced success. Everything he had done previously put him in the team and as a result he got lost in details that prevented him from building the structures he needed. He got caught up in the day-to-day customer challenges and missed the big picture. He had always wondered why he wasn't able to get a good idea off the ground. Then he discovered the six-minute workday principles and recognized many things he had never heard before. His previous business efforts didn't have a long-term plan of simplifying things and placing him as the conductor of the team. Immediately, he experienced positive results.

Armed with the new and effective strategies of the six-minute workday, Keith began to thrive. Soon he joined us at a mastermind event in Maui. He began to build his network and learn from other high-level entrepreneurs about his role as a leader and manager. Again his company expanded and the profits climbed. For the first time in his life, he became excited as his ideas now began to take root and his income soared.

He later wrote that sometimes it just takes a little clarity to fit within your own company.

Keith's biggest aha from the live training: "If you look at the word entrepreneur, it's a French word, so most people don't know where the letter u fits in exactly. This is like business for most. They don't know where 'u' fit. But once that's figured out, you can achieve amazing results."

Raymond was unsure of what kind of business he should get involved in. He knew that he was an entrepreneur at heart. He just didn't know where he fit. Then he discovered the five pillars. You may be surprised to learn that he didn't make his decision as to how to proceed based on selecting his favorite pillar. Instead, he looked at which ones he didn't really have an interest in and one of them that he actually had a fear about. Ultimately, he decided to build an enterprise around investing and the movement of money. He didn't have any experience around this idea but it intrigued him so he began to learn more about it and surround himself with others who knew.

As soon as he understood a significant way to create a transaction around money, he developed a strategy to become a hard money lender using other people's money. He used other experts to complete the legal requirements to both raise money and lend it out. In his first year in business, he loaned out just over $25 million. As a result, he has made some incredible profits, and with his growing support team *and team of investors and customers he has almost achieved a six-minute workday.*

Raymond's biggest aha from the live training: "The principle of building a safety net to support you has literally built my business. I always worried about what I didn't know until I realized that this was the wrong approach. Don't worry about what you don't know, worry about who you don't know. There is always an expert who can help you answer a question or even do the work for you to grow your business."

Talia had just graduated from community college, but she felt more confused than ever. What should she do with her life? She had experience for a few things, but as she finished, she realized that none of the things she had studied were really what she wanted to spend the rest of her life doing. She enjoyed her humanities classes and was fluent in Spanish, French, and English. She wanted the freedom to travel and explore and wasn't ready to settle down behind a desk at a nine-to-five.

She knew that her biggest challenge would be finding a way to feel fulfilled and yet make an income at the same time. She attended one of our live weekend events called "The Collaboration Conference" www.TheCollaboration Conference.com and met several students at a mastermind session who encouraged her to start a business around her interest in travel. She was adamant that she didn't want to become a travel agent. To her, that was another desk job. But as the group brainstormed, they came up with a genius idea for her. She could become an online review service for various resorts or activities. She wasn't sure how to monetize it or structure it, however, and was about to give up—until the members of her mastermind team started coming up with possibilities. In a short time, they identified some creative ways to not only fund the business but have it become highly profitable. They also worked out how a spectacular team could be built to support the entire program.

Talia now spends the majority of her time traveling under this new business model, and with her team she has achieved a six-minute workday.

Talia's biggest aha from the mastermind event was that "I always felt I was on my own to figure things out. I often gave up on ideas because I didn't think I was smart enough. My collaboration team has helped me to see better ways and has kept me moving forward. They are inspiring, but also make me accountable. It's just like Doug says: 'Your network becomes your safety net.'"

Ken's first words when I met him were, "Oops." He then revealed that he was in the middle of a massive repair attempt with a venture he had gotten a little too relaxed with. It was a brick-and-mortar company he had built almost a decade ago that provided plumbing services. He had a few employees, trucks, and even a building that he owned. But he had taken the flow of the company for granted and started taking more and more time off and letting everyone just do their own thing. Sometimes he justified himself by saying, "They are adults. And they are getting paid. So I can trust them to do what they need to do."

At first there were no indications that he needed to worry and Ken didn't make contact with his employees for weeks at a time while he enjoyed beaches in Mexico, Dominican Republic, and Cuba with his girlfriend. But after a while, the cracks became pretty obvious.

As we helped him through the repair process, he was thankfully able to not only keep his company together but expand it and make it more profitable. He still spends lots of time on the beaches of his choice, but now with the six-minute-workday strategies his company is thriving.

Ken once told me, "If it hadn't been for the structure that I learned specifically around reporting and training leaders, I think I would have been back to being a solopreneur driving my own truck and filling the appointments every day on my own."

Jarom was ready to give up. His first business failed in a dramatic way, leaving him in enormous debt. He had literally given everything he had and everything he could borrow to this venture. And it failed. With a new full-time job selling cars, he was torn by wanting to live his dream as an entrepreneur and trying to figure out how to keep his creditors happy.

As he encountered the six-minute-workday principles, he discovered the foundation of his business problem. The transaction hadn't been properly constructed, and as a result every encounter with a customer was different and could not be systematized. Without a system, he could not add any support mechanisms. He had created a situation where he had to reinvent his business model pretty much every time he encountered a new prospect.

Switching to part-time at the car dealership, Jarom returned to the company that he had created and reworked the transactions to be clear and predictable. He developed a pattern that could be followed every time and made it work with systems.

Within eight months of the original catastrophe, Jarom was able to escape the debt and leave the car dealership in pursuit of a six-minute workday.

Jarom shared his thoughts in an email. "I was so discouraged. I couldn't believe I failed. I borrowed money from my parents. I borrowed money from my grandparents. I borrowed money from an uncle and the bank. When I failed, I thought I was totally screwed. I even avoided going home and to family functions. But when I discovered what I was missing in my company, it was like I got hit by lightning. In a positive way, of course. I knew what I needed to do, and as soon as I started doing it, right things came together."

Jane had attended the six-minute workday live event. She had also been on one of our entrepreneur cruises through the Caribbean. She was a fun person who was considered the life of the party and always energetic. Everybody liked her. She was always involved in the masterminds and always extremely helpful with practical ideas. But I noticed that she was still working a full-time job. In one of the coaching sessions I asked her why she continued to work and to tell me a little about her venture that she was working on as her six-minute workday project.

Her smile quickly faded and she said that she didn't have a project and that she preferred to just be on the side and help others. As we talked about it, she said she didn't feel like she was ready to be an entrepreneur out on her own. She felt her calling in life was to simply help others who were entrepreneurs to fulfill their dream. "Couldn't that be your venture? A support service for entrepreneurs?"

Her mouth dropped. "That's it. OMG. I can't believe I didn't see this before." We spent the remainder of the coaching session working through the venture as if she were recommending to a third party how it should be built. Supporting others was her gift, after all.

Two months later, she was up and running and serving many of our students and others around the world as a top-notch consulting firm. And she does not do all the work herself. In fact, she has assembled a team of a dozen others who guide people through our process. Most likely you will meet her at our events, as she is now one of our Certified Six-Minute Workday Coaches.

Jane's feelings about us are obviously very positive. I feel as if I need to tone down what she says as it's almost a bit too much. But here's a note she wrote to me recently: "The six-minute workday saved my life. It gave me purpose. It gives me my power. It is my passion. If you are an entrepreneur and you are not using these strategies, you are operating well below your possibilities. Do yourself a massive favor right now and join this tribe. It will up-level your business and life like no other program on the earth. It is the very best there is."

Ryan was struggling with getting some clarity in his business. There were also lots of problems that he didn't know how to solve. He had hired consultants and business coaches, attended seminars, and read books. All of which were helpful but didn't give him what he needed to be fully successful. To confess, he even found it difficult for him to implement some of the six-minute-workday principles we taught him. But one thing did help—being mentored and supported by the same top achievers and entrepreneurs who had originally helped me.

At our programs I still invite those I learned from back when I conducted my original interviews with the world's top entrepreneurs. They come out in person and mentor, teach, and train our students at the live events, masterminds, cruises, and retreats.

At our events and trainings, we have had the founder of Reebok, the founder of UGG boots, one of the founders of FedEx, a cofounder of Ted Baker, a former CEO of Fruit of the Loom, marketing people from Uber, the creators of Chicken Soup for the Soul, and many others. When Ryan struggled, he simply sat with one of these top entrepreneurs at lunchtime. Together they worked through some of the problems Ryan was facing and came up with practical real-world solutions.

As far as I am aware, our events represent the only functions in the world where you can have access to this kind of power at close proximity. I am not talking about what you see at other events where you pay to get a photo with someone. I am talking about real one-on-one conversations. They happen in our tribe.

Ryan has continued to bond with many of our top entrepreneurs and they continue to be a support for him. Ryan's situation is not uncommon, as you'll find out when you come and join us.

Ryan shared the following: "The biggest value that I continue to receive is that, whenever I have a problem, I can actually reach out to one of the top entrepreneur mentors and get answers. Most of them are personal contacts on my cell phone. They are interested in my success and have made themselves accessible to me when I need them. They care about my success."

ACKNOWLEDGMENTS

I want to acknowledge the following people for their support and help in making this project possible. Firstly, our team: Kristi Maggie, Ash Ahern, Adam Ceres, Jay Larracas, Tyler Basu, Rachel Dobson, and direct assistant Marian Clarissa Medina. Thanks to the book team, especially my agent, Bill Gladstone, and Matt Holt and the team at BenBella. I also want to acknowledge the support from my family and friends. There are far too many of you to list, but I love you all.

ABOUT THE AUTHOR

Douglas Vermeeren has personally interviewed more than four hundred of the world's top business leaders, CEOs, and founders from companies like Nike, Reebok, Fruit of the Loom, FedEx, American Airlines, Microsoft, UGG boots, Uber, KFC, Apple, McDonald's, Disney, Sony, United Airlines, Ted Baker, Toyota, Kajabi, and others to share their success secrets with you. ABC television and Fox Business refer to him as the modern-day Napoleon Hill.

Photo by Trevor Carter,
D'Angelo Photography, Calgary

Douglas has authored three books in the Guerrilla Marketing series. He is a regular featured expert on FOX, CNN, ABC, NBC, CTV, and CBC, among others.

His six-minute workday training programs share strategies on how to think, act, and build business at high levels and keep your time. He is also known as a top connector and teaches others how to connect with the highest-level achievers and expand your network to grow your business.

His award-winning entrepreneur & wealth training programs have been rated among the best in the world.

www.DouglasVermeeren.com

www.SixMinuteWorkday.com

As a side note, he is also the director and producer of four of the top ten personal development movies today.

JOIN US FOR SUPPORT

Thank you for joining us in this book. I have enjoyed sharing these principles with you and I sincerely hope that you have been inspired to start building your new venture.

However, I must confess that after having taught this material to students on nearly every continent around the globe, there are some people who succeed incredibly with this information while others struggle and don't get anywhere.

The ones who succeed create sustainable income models in their life and most of them very quickly cut their work time in half. Soon after that, they reduce their workday by greater and greater increments until they are so productive that they, too, start living a six-minute workday every day.

One of the most important shifts that successful entrepreneurs make to get the most out of this material and arrive at sustainable results was spoken of in the final chapter on what to do next. The point that I am talking about is becoming immersed in this content.

I can always tell how successful someone will be by their level of commitment. It goes without saying that the most committed person gets the very best results.

If you're serious about your commitment to become a high-level, organized entrepreneur leading a highly profitable company and doing it in only six minutes a day, I want to help you. Here are some of the ways you can become immersed in this material and increase the chances of your success.

Live & Online Trainings: Our teams host regular trainings both live and online. Some of these trainings consist of multiple live events where I am joined by several top-achieving entrepreneur guests who unfold their tactics and systems for success in today's marketplace. These events are focused on giving you tangible, relevant, and applicable skills for building businesses in the real world. Many of these events have breakout sessions and special VIP access to multimillionaire and billionaire business leaders.

One-on-One or Group Coaching: Coaching is a proven way to accelerate your success. There are options for every level of experience. We have incredible Certified Six-Minute Workday Coaches and senior entrepreneur coaches. I still do some coaching as well, but I should warn you I currently have a three-year waiting list.

Retreats & Masterminds: These are power-learning and networking opportunities. We host masterminds and business retreats through the year. Not to mention that these can be tax-deductible trips for your business. At these retreats, not only will you experience the six-minute lifestyle in all its luxury, but you will also have the opportunity to build powerful high-level relationships.

The Collaboration Conference: This invite-only conference connects high-level entrepreneurs with the intention to create powerful outcomes through collaboration. Feel free to complete an application to attend and you may just be invited to this exclusive event.

Become a Six-Minute Workday Certified Coach: Business coaching or entrepreneur consulting is a quickly growing industry, and there are many well-meaning business coaches in the marketplace today who are trying their best to help. However, the lessons they have been teaching are often incomplete. As I spent over a decade learning directly from the world's top entrepreneurs and business leaders, I discovered several lessons that aren't being taught today. And as I built my first million-dollar enterprise, I discovered how these lessons actually fit into place in a real-life context. The tools you will learn in the six-minute-workday program are above anything else that I have seen available today. I believe that if more business coaches had these tools to share with their clients, ventures would prosper and amazing things would happen for small businesses everywhere. For this reason, we have decided it is essential to start giving the coaches that guide business an opportunity to level up their skills. Not only should they have a prosperous venture of their own as evidence that they understand these principles but they should have the connection to the same top business leaders that I did. *Business success isn't just about knowing what to do; it's also having the right network to help you do it.*

If you are a business coach that wants to become more valuable to your clients and experience more personal success, we have a special certification program designed for you to become more prosperous and effective and to help others do the same. Reach out to us for details.

Coupon

$500 FOR PARTICIPATION IN ANY OF THE ABOVE